The Agile Manager's Guide To

MOTIVATING PEOPLE

The Agile Manager's Guide To

MOTIVATING PEOPLE

By Joseph T. Straub

Velocity Business Publishing
Bristol, Vermont USA

Copyright © 1997, 2001 by Joseph T. Straub

Second Edition, Expanded

All Rights Reserved

ISBN 1-58099-030-4

Title page illustration by Elayne Sears

Printed in Canada

If you'd like additional copies of this book or a catalog of books in the Agile Manager Series®, please get in touch with us.

- **Write us at:**
Velocity Business Publishing, Inc.
15 Main Street
Bristol, VT 05443 USA

- **Call us at:**
1-888-805-8600 in North America (toll-free)
1-802-453-6669 from all other countries

- **Fax us at:**
1-802-453-2164

- **E-mail us at:**
action@agilemanager.com

- **Visit our Web site at:**
www.agilemanager.com

The Web site contains much of interest to business people—tips and techniques, and downloadable versions of titles in the Agile Manager Series.

For Pat and Stacey
Your love is my greatest motivator

Contents

Books in the Agile Manager Series®:

Introduction

You really need John to stay late to finish a report that's due in the morning. Not looking you in the eye, he says, "I can't tonight. I . . . uh . . . have to go to a school function."

Kim, whom you inherited from a predecessor, is habitually late for work. Yet she constantly badgers you for time off for this and that and acts hurt and lowers her output when you don't give in.

Ray's a real menace. He's a competent worker, but you know he constantly sneers at you and other managers behind your backs. His mere presence lowers everyone's morale.

Aubrey is a happy-go-lucky chap who's fun to have around. And he's bright. Yet he does only the bare minimum to get by. Why won't he give more of himself?

"Is it me?" you wonder. "Is it our operating systems? Or the organization?"

As this book will show, it could be all three. Your approach to motivating people may need fine-tuning—or an outright overhaul. Or your operating systems may degrade people or leave them feeling unappreciated. Finally, your organizational culture may turn otherwise good folk into parasites who delight in undermining the work of others or avoiding even a hint of responsibility.

This book will help you correct all three situations. It'll explain why people behave as they do, plus offer a dozen or more practical techniques you can use on the job today to get the results you want.

But after reading this book, "the results you want" may change. If you've been looking for a bigger stick to whack people with, you may discover here a technique that instead provides a juicier, sweeter carrot to entice people to act in ways that better benefit the organization.

Or you may realize that you can improve results by asking for the input of those who will carry out the work. Or you may recast your view of the people who work for you—you may begin to see capabilities in them you never knew existed.

In short, be prepared to broaden your thinking about what it takes to move people in beneficial directions. Doing that alone will get you better results. Broadening your thinking *and* applying the methods contained in this book can result in large leaps in productivity.

The Agile Manager's Guide to Motivating People is designed to go down easily. You'll read it in a few sittings, then have it nearby to refer to when necessary. For managers with people problems, it'll prove a lifesaver.

★   ★   ★

A note on the "Reality Checks." You'll find a number of Reality Checks—real-world experiences and quips—in each chapter. They're intended both to lighten things up and to confirm the maxim, "Managers are never worthless. Some can always be used as bad examples."

The source of these anecdotes are experiences I've had as a manager or heard about firsthand over the years.

Chapter One

Motivation: Who Needs It?

"The journey to the future is easier if you look forward instead of backward."

ANONYMOUS

The Agile Manager was just about to round a corner when he heard Wanda, his second-in-command, speaking with more ice in her voice than he'd ever heard.

"I need the drawings for the prototype," she said. "And I need them tomorrow. I don't care what you have planned for this evening. I want them tomorrow!"

"Fine," came the dispirited response. The Agile Manager, still hidden, identified the voice as that of William, one of the product developers in his department.

"Good," said Wanda, softening ever so slightly. "I think that's a smart move on your part. I don't understand why—"

She stopped as the Agile Manager suddenly strode into view with a big smile on his face.

"Hi y'all," he said in a fake Southern accent. William stared at

11

the floor, looking hopelessly depressed. "Hey Wanda," he said, "I need to talk to you about something. Let's go to my office."

After they'd settled into a couple of chairs, the Agile Manager asked, "What was that all about?"

"William's a slacker," she said with a sour look. "If these kids worried less about what they were going to do each evening and more about work, we'd get a lot more done around here. Can you believe that guy still plays 'Jails and Warlords'? And he's, what, twenty-seven?"

I bet that makes him more creative, thought the Agile Manager. "Wanda," he said, "William and Manuel and a few of the younger people have a different outlook on life than you or I, no doubt about it. But complaining about it won't do any good. They'll never be like us. Besides, I think Will is pretty creative. And I've seen him work as hard as anyone during crunch periods. When he's into a project, he eats, drinks, and breathes it."

"Well I wish he was into the rework of the 1800B," said Wanda.

"I've got a challenge for you," replied the Agile Manager. "The challenge is for you to reach William somehow and get him excited about that job. He'll be on it for a couple of months, so you need his best efforts."

"How will I do that?" asked Wanda, genuinely puzzled.

"You figure it out. My only tip is that you need to engage his interests . . ."

"Motivation is doing more than you have to." That's the working definition we'll use throughout this book.

Agile managers invest more than the average amount of energy, enthusiasm, time, and effort in their work, and they constantly look for ways to motivate their employees to do likewise. They see themselves and their workers as exceptional people.

This doesn't mean they're conceited, smug, or holier-than-thou. They simply believe, and live the belief, that they are not run-of-the-mill. This deep-rooted dedication to excellence is reflected in their goals, thoughts, words, and actions. Mediocrity? That's for those who are content with less than the best.

Who Needs Motivation?

You and your employees alike need motivating. Motivation applies to:

- Your relationships with employees. It's part of every manager's job to ensure that workers invest more of themselves in their work than they absolutely must.
- Your relationship with yourself. You need an inventory of techniques and "tricks of the trade" that you can employ to move yourself off dead-center for the sake of your own future.

One the oldest definitions of management is "getting things done through others," and your employees are a major group of those "others." Most of this book deals with your role in motivating them, because so much of your reputation and success depends on how effectively and productively your people perform.

Reality Check

A nasty boss who ran an apple orchard would visit a particular orchard a few times a day. Whenever he came, he'd whip out a stopwatch and time the apple pickers. If they fell short of what he believed they were capable of picking in an hour, he'd berate them mercilessly.

Productivity was low, yet every time the boss showed up, the workers looked busy. That angered him even more.

Volume was low because the apple-picking crew, sick of the constant verbal beatings, posted a worker atop an apple tree on a knoll to act as lookout. When the boss wasn't around, the crew lolled around.

When the boss's truck approached, the lookout gave a signal and everyone began to work industriously. When he left, they slacked off again.

The nasty boss never understood that, short of standing over them with a gun, you can't force people to be productive.

You have to figure out methods to get people to do what you want them to because *they* want to do it. That's not an easy task, because each person is different. But this book will show you where to start.

It's equally important for you to know how to motivate yourself. Your boss may not take the time and trouble—no matter how many copies of this book you leave on his or her desk—to do for you what you, as an agile manager, have resolved to do for your own workers.

Best Tip

Be aware: Negative motivators generate smoldering rage, contempt, and resentment of titanic proportions.

Self-motivation is an intriguing, useful topic, and one that's rarely mentioned in motivational seminars and books. So rarely, in fact, that I haven't seen it mentioned at all, except in an interview with a management writer and consultant about eight years ago. That guy was me. I'm just itching to get into the subject, and we will a little bit later. It's fun to explore.

Self-help books have been written about hundreds of topics, yet few, if any, actually deal with the need to motivate yourself. That's strange, because when it comes to self-improvement and success, self-motivation is the nucleus of it all.

As one down-home agile manager put it, "You've got to have the want-to first." So if you want to have the want-to, but aren't sure how to get it, chapter five will show you how.

Negative Motivators Don't Prosper

Our working definition of motivation actually leaves room for two kinds: positive and negative.

Negative motivation is all around us. Everyone can recall some bitter and unpleasant experiences with it, whether at home, in school, or at work (and probably all three). Yes, managers may be able to force, browbeat, or intimidate employees into perform-

---

Reality Check

A worker had just met a next-to-impossible deadline. Her boss said, "Remember when I told you that you could either get this system up and running by today or update your résumé? Who says threats are counterproductive?!"

---

ing above the average, but only for a short time.

It's a terrible idea.

Negative motivators, no matter where we meet them, generate smoldering rage, contempt, and resentment of titanic proportions. Penalties and threats may produce a quick fix for performance problems, but they provide no enduring solution.

Managers who resort to negative motivation ultimately generate many more problems for themselves and their organizations than they're trying to solve. Moreover, they'd best sleep with one eye open, figuratively speaking. The people on the receiving end of their miserable, misguided, and boneheaded efforts will gleefully sabotage their reputations, careers, and accomplishments—and escape from their control at the first opportunity.

Ready, Set, Go!

This book is going to look at principles and techniques of positive motivation. We'll start by exploring three popular motivational theories that have been around for many years. Then we'll profile a variety of positive motivational programs and practices that you can apply either on your own or as part of widespread or comprehensive programs within your organization.

Best Tip

Penalties and threats provide no enduring solution to performance problems.

By the time you finish this book, you'll agree that motivation—the positive variety—is a major piece of the management puzzle. The ability to get people to give more of themselves than they must is a powerful one.

And it goes a long way toward establishing your reputation as a manager who gets results.

The Agile Manager's Checklist

✔ Positive motivation is doing "more than you have to."
✔ To achieve the best results, concern yourself with motivating your employees—and yourself.
✔ While you can browbeat or intimidate employees into performing above average, it only works for a short time.
✔ In business, good motivators go far.

Chapter Two

*P*opular Theories of Motivation

"Managements have always looked at man as an animal to be manipulated with a carrot and a stick. They found that when a man hurts, he will move to avoid pain—and they say, 'We're motivating the employees.' Hell, you're not motivating them, you're moving them."

FREDERICK HERZBERG, PROFESSOR EMERITUS, UNIVERSITY OF UTAH

"People don't change their behavior unless it makes a difference for them to do so."

FRAN TARKENTON, CONSULTANT AND FORMER PRO FOOTBALL PLAYER

Wanda leafed through an article on Abraham Maslow that the Agile Manager had given her without comment.
She considered William in light of Maslow's Hierarchy of Needs.
He's paid well and he knows his job is reasonably secure, she thought. And considering his best friends work here, he's got social needs covered.

Self-esteem needs? Hmm. I don't know much of what he does outside the office besides play silly games and spend money to have fun. Do I have an obligation to help him meet his esteem or self-fulfillment needs? And what about—

At that moment, William knocked on her open door and walked in. "Here," he said, his voice flat, handing her a folder. "The drawings." He turned and walked out.

"Thanks," said Wanda, wondering whether to call him back in. She thought, I do have a problem, don't I? I don't know what part I had in creating it, but I'm surely the one who has to solve it.

The theories of motivation explained in this chapter are the ones you always envied. The really, really cool ones. They dressed sharp, always seemed to have plenty of money, and hung out in all the right places. The other theories wanted to be like them. Now, years later, after they've become legendary and lived up to their reputations, they're still talked about at every Theory Reunion. We introduce, ladies and gentlemen (drum roll), Douglas McGregor, Frederick Herzberg, and Abraham Maslow.

DOUGLAS McGREGOR: THEORY X AND THEORY Y

Some wise guy once said there are two general categories of people: those who categorize people and those who don't. Douglas McGregor put a different spin on this by declaring that there are two categories of managers: Theory X managers and Theory Y managers.

Theory X

McGregor said that a Theory X boss believes people are basically lazy. They're untrustworthy and must be watched with all the intensity of a satyr eyeing a virgin. They only work for money. A Theory X boss's motto might be, "I'm paid to think. You're paid to work. And I'm going to stand over you to make sure you do." (Did that just describe some of your ex-bosses? I thought so!)

Theory Y

But how about a Theory Y boss? According to McGregor, Theory Y bosses believe the opposite of Theory Xers. These managers believe that people *do* want more than money from their jobs. They can be trusted. They can be self-managing. They don't need someone breathing down their necks all the time (at least after they've learned their jobs and gotten their feet on the ground).

A Theory Y boss compliments people by believing they can do more than even *they* think they can. To some workers, especially those who lack self-confidence or are afraid to try their wings (perhaps because they've been clipped by Theory X managers in the past), that belief can be one of the greatest motiva-

---

Reality Check

The boss of a nonprofit housing organization loved to start new initiatives while ignoring the details of running the organization.

In a typically grand plan, he decided he wanted to build a complex of buildings for low-income people. As he well knew, however, this was a make-or-break project for the organization. If any part of it failed, the organization would fail.

A good boss would work board members, using good arguments based on logic and fact, to get them aligned behind his vision.

A bad boss would keep the board in the dark and then spring the plan at the last possible minute, when it was too late to go back. And he wouldn't even hint at the financial or organizational risks involved.

A really bad boss would do that and worse. The hero of our story convened a last-minute board meeting and then made an unprepared employee stand up and explain and defend the plan. The boss sat idly by as he took the heat.

tors and most flattering compliments of all. A Theory Y boss's motto might be "We're paid to think and work together."

What does all this boil down to? Maybe this: People tend to feed back to their bosses the same behavior and attitude those bosses expect. If you expect your employees to be lazy, no-good bums who would make the Three Stooges look like rocket scientists, can't wait until payday, and will goof off every time you turn your back, you sure don't give them any reasons to do otherwise.

On the other hand, if you expect the best from your people— positive attitudes; responsible, exceptional performance; and conscientious, ethical, customer- or team-oriented behavior— they'll usually bust their butts not to disappoint you.

| Best Tip

If you expect good things from your employees, and give them the tools to succeed, they'll do you proud.

It's a matter of expectations. Theory X bosses expect people to live down to their negative expectations and virtually encourage them to. These managers (who are about as agile as an iceberg) might say, "I'm afraid you'll fail, so I won't let you try. I don't trust you, I don't think you want to better yourself, and you'll always be a loser."

Meanwhile, elsewhere in the office, there are (we hope) upbeat Theory Y managers who expect people to live up to their positive expectations by saying (with words and actions), "I believe you want to do a good job. I believe you're looking for an opportunity to try, and I'm willing to take a chance by giving you a chance. I don't think you'll disappoint either of us."

In an even tighter nutshell, McGregor believed that managers tend to reap the kind of behavior, performance, and attitudes they sow.

To put this in a nonmanagement setting, think about your parents or the parents of anyone you've been close to. Bad expectations versus good ones can have as deep and enduring an impact on children as on employees. (This isn't to equate your employees with children, of course. For one thing, your employees probably wear larger shoes and have learned not to run with scissors.)

FREDERICK HERZBERG: HYGIENE AND MOTIVATION

You met Herzberg briefly in one of this chapter's opening quotes. He believed that people's work and workplace have a major impact on their motivation.

Herzberg contended that jobs consist of two sets of factors: maintenance or "hygiene" factors, and motivational factors. Let's look at each type.

Maintenance Factors

Maintenance factors are the basic things that employees feel they have a right to get no matter where they work. They're part of the work environment. You could list them yourself if you thought about it:

- *Adequate pay.* When you look at your paycheck, your blood pressure doesn't skyrocket. You don't feel that you're being ripped off or taken advantage of.
- *Satisfactory working conditions.* The furniture and climate controls are comfortable, the copy machine doesn't break down every time it sees you coming, and you have the resources (time, space, budget, equipment, and people) that you need to do your job well.
- *Decent fringe benefits.* Your employer provides a competitive life and health insurance plan, paid vacations, employee discounts, work breaks, and the like.
- *An acceptable working relationship with your boss.* Your manager respects you, and the two of you tend to get along most of the time.

So there you have it—a basic inventory of entitlements that

people feel they have a right to wherever they work. If they don't get 'em, they get really agitated and believe they're getting screwed. (Or, as Herzberg put it, they're "dissatisfied.")

If they can find a job that supplies more of these maintenance factors, they'll probably lay rubber out of the employees' parking lot like a dragon in heat.

Remember, though, that if they do get them, they're not satisfied—they're simply not *dis*satisfied.

Giving people what they believe they're entitled to, however, sure as heck won't cause them to put more of themselves into their jobs than they're required to. Hardly a surprise, huh? Who was ever motivated by fair treatment? Treating people right won't move them to invest more of themselves in their work than they really have to.

Motivational Factors

Motivational factors are the things that make people willing to work beyond the boundaries of their job descriptions, go the extra mile, and reach beyond their grasp in genuine Rocky Balboa fashion. They include a chance to be promoted, the opportunity to grow within the present job, receiving praise for a job well done, and having work that you fundamentally like and look forward to doing.

Motivational factors are found in the job itself. If they're

Reality Check

Ready, fire, aim!

Worker: "The deadline for this job is next to impossible! We've got to develop a time line, create checkpoints, and set up a PERT chart that links everything together in a logical action plan—and all within the next day or two."

Boss: "Are you crazy? We don't have time to sit around planning! We've just got to jump in and do it!"

present, workers are satisfied. If they're absent, workers won't be *dis*satisfied—that is, they won't necessarily line up to quit (as they would if they had lousy pay, subhuman working conditions, and the rest of Herzberg's maintenance factors)—but neither will they do more than they must.

Herzberg's message to managers, then, might be:

➜ Design your company's jobs to provide built-in challenges that call on workers to develop new employability skills, apply their ingenuity, and grow as individuals without having to be promoted. Individual managers can even do some of this by giving employees the opportunity to take on special projects, work on new proposals, critique and recommend changes in existing systems or procedures, or represent the department on internal and external committees and task forces. People may also welcome the chance to attend company-sponsored courses and seminars and engage in other activities that would improve the scope of their knowledge and abilities.

|Best Tip

Good pay and working conditions don't satisfy people— they only keep them from feeling *dissatisfied*.

➜ Higher executives must set goals and lead the organization from the top in a fashion that generates opportunities for people to move up the ladder (easier said than done, I know, in these times of downsizing).

➜ Acknowledge work well done. People know when they deserve a pat on the back, and they'll expect you to deliver it and say "thank you." But make sure it really is work well done.

According to *Forbes* magazine, General Motors devised a program in the mid-1980s to pay workers $50 for every three months of perfect attendance and an additional $300 for perfect attendance all year. The plan cost the company $400 million, but absenteeism didn't drop at all. Why? Because $50 a quarter wasn't that big a deal compared to employees' regular wages, and only about 5 percent of the company's workers were regularly absent.

The program was actually paying the other 95 percent of the workforce for doing what they tended to do anyway, while giving workers the impression that regular attendance and responsible behavior were things that deserved to be rewarded.

➡ Hire smart! People who enjoy the work they've been hired to do are prone to do it better. (You'll hear more about this later.)

You and your organization must cover both maintenance and motivational factors. Providing one or the other won't cut it. Giving workers only the basic maintenance or hygiene factors will cause them to stick around, but they won't be motivated to do more than reach for the pinnacle of mediocrity.

Likewise, if you give them only motivational factors and ignore the maintenance factors, they'll quit. They'll believe they're getting a raw deal.

Herzberg's two sets of factors are thus complementary and interdependent. You've gotta give people the yo-yo and the string, the car and the keys, the knife and the fork.

ABRAHAM MASLOW'S
HIERARCHY OF NEEDS

Abraham Maslow didn't disagree with McGregor and Herzberg. He just took a different view. As in the fable of the three blind men describing an elephant (one pictured it as a rope, another as a tree trunk, the third as a house), each of these fellows had his own view, and none of them is necessarily "right" or "wrong." (Or, in the elephant example, none is pachydermically challenged.)

Maslow's view looked beyond the limits of the supervisor or job, however. He contended that people have a hierarchy of five needs that they try to satisfy, and these needs range from the most basic to the most complex.

Physiological Needs

These are needs for food, drink, and shelter. They're as basic as you get. If your back's really to the wall, you might even commit homicide to satisfy them.

A job has the potential to cover them if it pays enough to buy food and shelter. Once you know you can cover these physiological needs whenever they come up (by having enough money to go through McDonald's drive-in lane, for example), it dawns on you that there's another, more complex need level above them.

Safety Needs

These include not only physical safety—that is, to go climb a tree or hole up in a cave after you've got enough to eat and drink—but also *psychological* safety, which comes with reasonable job security, and the more the better. If you've talked to anybody whose company has downsized lately, you know how powerful this need is!

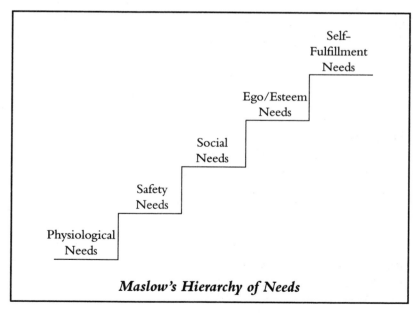

Maslow's Hierarchy of Needs

Many organizations have been formed and many laws have been passed to try to cover the safety needs of employees and/or consumers. In the U.S., these include, for example, labor unions, the American Arbitration Association, the Federal Mediation and Conciliation Service, the Occupational Safety and Health Act, the Food and Drug Administration, and the National Institute of Safety and Health.

Moreover, incidents of holdups, robberies, and workplace violence by both disgruntled customers and co-workers (i.e., "going postal") have spurred both management and worker efforts to provide a physically safe workplace.

Social Needs

Okay, do you have the first two need levels covered? Congratulations, but you're not done yet. You have social needs—needs for love, affection, and acceptance. Just be careful how you try to satisfy these needs at work. You might get slapped with a sexual-harassment lawsuit.

A job may cover a worker's physiological and safety needs fairly well if the pay is OK and there's adequate physical and psychological security. ("OK" and "adequate" are highly subjective measures, of course.) But social needs? A job can help to cover these if you get along well with your co-workers, party off the job with them, and enjoy relating to your colleagues on a social as well as a professional level.

One of the greatest jobs I ever had that covered these needs very well was a summer job running a miniature golf course. It was part of a bar, restaurant, and beachwear complex on Clearwater Beach, Florida. Most of my co-workers were fraternity brothers. We could eat free all day, drink beer at cost after closing up at night, come to work in Bermuda shorts and T-shirts, and hit on the young ladies who walked by on their way to the beach—which was only fifty yards away. Social needs covered big time!

If your job doesn't give you much social satisfaction (please accept my sympathy), Maslow said you'll try to cover your social needs in other places and through other relationships.

Esteem Needs

These are sometimes called ego needs, and everybody has them. We need to feel a sense of identity, achievement, accomplishment, worth, and value.

It's no surprise that a job may cover these needs to different degrees with different people—and not at all for some.

Sometimes I've talked with managers who are baffled about a certain employee's behavior. "I just don't understand Smedley," one might say. "She's not going to be fired, but she's no ball of fire, either. She could really be a top performer if she would work up to her potential. When she leaves the office, though, I know that she does volunteer work for the Red Cross, coaches a Little League team, and has written the definitive biography of the widow of the Unknown Soldier. Why doesn't she invest some of that incredible energy and enthusiasm here?"

Best Tip

Hire smart. People who enjoy the work they do will do it both better and faster.

The answer sometimes is that Smedley's work experience doesn't wind her watch. She doesn't feel valuable and important doing whatever it is she does at work.

That "work experience," by the way, includes her manager as well as the corporate culture that radiates down from the folks in the executive suite. (Some of whom, of course, may feel the same as Smedley, only their paychecks are larger and they can eat in the executive dining room.)

Symbolically, Smedley may be saying—whether she realizes it or not—"I'm damn sure going to find something to do that makes me feel that my life's not wasted, and when I find it, get out of my way!"

A manager in my car pool some years ago looked wistfully

out the car window as we left the parking lot one day and saw a groundskeeper cutting grass with a lawn mower. "What a great job," he murmured. "Why?" I asked, knowing he probably made five times more than the groundskeeper. "Because at the end of the day I could at least look behind me and see where I'd been."

Several years ago, one of my textbook editors told me about another author who had become burned out and demotivated near the end of a lengthy book project. The manuscript was several chapters short of being done, and there wasn't enough time to line up a ghostwriter or coauthor to finish the job.

The editor went to his company's art director and said, "We've got to design the cover of this book now, even though it's not finished yet. If we can show the author his book cover, with his name on it, I think it'll get him pumped up and moving again."

This tactic, which appealed very strongly to the writer's esteem and self-fulfillment needs, had the desired effect. He cranked up his word processor and completed the rest of the manuscript so the publisher could launch the book on schedule.

Self-Fulfillment Needs

To borrow the U.S. Army slogan, this is the need to "Be all that you can be." People are only aware of it after Maslow's first four needs are covered, however.

When you hit this level, you're getting all you can from that great experience called life. Maslow figured that only about 10 percent of the population feels truly self-fulfilled at any one time. Part of the reason is that many of the experiences, relationships, and achievements that really make you feel like a complete and fulfilled person today probably won't make you feel that way next year.

Why? Because the novelty wears off. Then people tend to start looking around for more invigorating challenges and fresh experiences, assuming that the first four lower-level needs remain covered.

I once knew an auto dealer who seemed to have the world by

the tail on a downhill pull. He ran a thriving business, was a high-profile community leader, and starred in his own television commercials. The guy seemed to have it all. But deep down, he wasn't satisfied.

What did he do? Among many other things, he went back to college for a doctorate, earned an instrument rating on his twin-engine airplane, set up a program with a nearby university to anonymously finance the education of capable-but-needy stu-

---

Reality Check

All three prototypes of an aerospace firm's newly designed missiles exploded during testing, and the company feared that the military would cancel the contract.

Engineers isolated the problem in one specific electronic assembly, and a team of higher managers went down to the production area to investigate.

As managers often do, they began by grilling the department manager and supervisors. After a few minutes, one of the more perceptive executives walked over to the assembly line where the part was built and started chatting with a production worker.

"I guess you know we've had some troubles with these," he said.

"We sure have," she replied. "I'm really worried. If the company loses this contract, I might be out of a job."

"Do you have any idea what the problem might be?"

"Yes, I do. It's this component right here. I'm installing it backwards."

"Ah, would you mind telling me why?"

"Well, I've been doing this job for a long time, so I've got a pretty good idea of what's right and what's not. When the new drawings came down, they called for this part to be put in backwards. I told my supervisor that the drawings had a mistake, but he told me to mind my own business and go by the book."

dents, and ran for the state legislature.

One of life's most gratifying challenges can consist of finding new and more rewarding goals or experiences to pursue. Self-fulfillment leads to self-renewal, and thank God it does. When we don't grow, we die.

On a personal note, self-fulfillment, along with several of Maslow's lower-level needs, is what drove yours truly to go from career gas station attendant to college graduate, production planning management trainee, production planning manager, graduate student, college professor, freelance management writer (who pens horror/suspense novels and short stories as time permits), amateur gourmet cook, and restorer of a '76 Datsun 280-Z. In the words of Teddy Roosevelt, "Life should be led like a cavalry charge."

Yet, as I write these words, two trash collectors are emptying the garbage cans at the curb in front of my home. And while I'm grateful for the combination of circumstances that placed us on different sides of the window, can I safely assume that I'm more self-fulfilled or content than they? I don't know.

Now that I've clarified Maslow's hierarchy, let's hit a few key points that I alluded to earlier. You must satisfy the needs in this hierarchy in order, from top to bottom, to really play it safe. If you shortchange or detour around any one of them to reach for a higher one, you're running a big risk.

> **Best Tip**
>
> Just because you feel fulfilled now doesn't mean you will in six months. To stay motivated, seek new challenges.

Take, for example, the kid who works in a gas station for minimum wage. He sleeps in the back room with the guard dog at night because he can't afford a place to live (physiological needs not met), and the owner grumbles ominously that business is bad (safety needs in jeopardy). Nevertheless, he goes down to Friendly Finance and manages to swing a loan to buy a fourth-hand Mustang GT 5-speed to im-

---

Reality Check

Top executive to staff, on reviewing an office's productivity in spite of a major layoff: "If we downsized that office by 20 percent and it's managed to do such a great job so soon, we obviously didn't cut deeply enough. We ought to be able to get rid of a dozen or so more, don't you think?"

---

press his friends with (grasping to satisfy an esteem need).

But what happens if he gets laid off? Friendly Finance repossesses the Mustang, assuming he hasn't totaled it, so his esteem needs go up in smoke. He's probably more concerned at this point, though, about beating the bricks to find another job.

Jobs and Maslow

Can someone's work satisfy every level on Maslow's hierarchy? Hardly. Oh, you do have your hard-charging eighty-hour-a-week workaholics, well-paid and staggering under the weight of status symbols, who seem to build everything in their lives around their careers. They may even draw up an organization chart to depict their family relationships (guess who's the CEO).

But such folks are rare, and some would say that they lead very narrow lives. A job may meet the first two needs fairly well if the pay is enough to cover the worker's physiological needs and there's reasonable physical and psychological safety, but its need-satisfying ability tends to taper off as you rise toward the top of the hierarchy.

Yet the more that someone's work helps to cover the top three needs in Maslow's hierarchy, the more motivated the worker may be to invest additional effort in the job.

That's an opportunity for agile managers. A job's design, a corporation's culture, and your behavior can all unite to help someone's work cover more of Maslow's higher-order needs than it otherwise might.

If the job doesn't cover these needs, people pursue hobbies, avocations, second jobs, or take early retirement to launch a second career to help satisfy their esteem and self-fulfillment needs.

It's also true that an identical experience can help to satisfy different needs for different people and contribute to some needs simultaneously. For example, a pay increase might help a minimum wage worker to cover physiological needs better and start contributing to a 401-K plan, whereas a raise for a corporate vice president might help only to satisfy her esteem needs. As one senior manager put it, "Once you get past a certain level, salary is just a way of keeping score."

I knew one executive, already earning a comfortable six-figure salary, who was being recruited by a competing company. The deal hinged on a difference of $100 per month between what he wanted and what they offered. Ego needs were the sticking point there.

Remember, too, that this hierarchy is as personal for priests as it is for Hell's Angels. What satisfies a priest's esteem needs (a promotion to cardinal, perhaps) may have no value to a biker (who might prefer to have the Harley-Davidson logo tattooed on his or her back).

With the analysis of what makes people tick on and off the job now finished, let's turn next to ways you can use your newfound theoretical knowledge to motivate people.

The Agile Manager's Checklist

✔ Expect the best from employees. They usually won't disappoint you.

✔ Beyond offering employees decent pay, offer them opportunities to grow and advance.

✔ Create a crack team of productive employees by helping them satisfy esteem and self-fulfillment needs on the job.

Chapter Three

Basic Practices That Motivate

*"The only way I can get you to do anything
is by giving you what you want."*

DALE CARNEGIE, WRITER AND PUBLIC-SPEAKING TEACHER

"William," said Wanda with all the warmth she could muster. "You did a fantastic job with those drawings. I don't see a single flaw in them. Thank you very much."

William sat speechless for a moment. "Thanks," he finally mumbled.

"I wonder," continued Wanda, "if you'd like to help me out. With our decision to add six new products this year, I'm really swamped. Would you like to take over the 1800B project altogether?"

William's eyes lit up. "Really? I'd love to," he said enthusiastically. "But what does that mean?"

"Well, said Wanda, "you'll be in charge from top to bottom. That means, first and foremost, that it's your responsibility to make sure it gets to market on time and without flaws." She eyed him

33

carefully to see how he took this. He didn't flinch. "You'll gather the right people on a team," she continued, "talk to me or the boss about the resources you'll need, call meetings, and bang on people who aren't producing. In a nice way, of course."
"Yes, yes, yes," Will said. "Starting now?"
"Starting now."
"Thanks, Wanda. You know," he began, eyeing her closely, "I didn't think you thought much of my abilities. Maybe you're still unsure. I'll show you what I can do, though. You won't be sorry."
Wanda smiled and walked away. I hope not, she thought.

In chapter two you got acquainted with the beliefs of some of the heaviest hitters in the field of motivation, but theory and practice work different sides of the street. How can an agile manager put chapter two's theories to work? That's the subject of these next two chapters.

Sound Hiring: The Key Prerequisite

Before any manager can hope to motivate any employee, there must be a sound match between the worker and the work. Clear, detailed job descriptions and job specifications can help you here. How can you hope to match up people and jobs compat-ibly without knowing what those jobs require in terms of experience, education, temperament, problem-solving and human-relations skills, and a host of other factors?

Best Tip
Expect even your best employees to change their interests, goals, and priorities every few years.

In addition, you have to complement your written job descriptions and specifications with a sound hiring procedure that helps to keep you from employing square pegs to work in round holes. Few management experiences are more frustrating and unpleasant than trying to motivate workers in jobs that they basically hate.

> ### *Reality Check*
>
> A senior manager escorted a group of college professors through an aerospace plant. He described what happened at each step in the production process like so:
> "Here's where I build the wiring harnesses for my missiles."
> "Here's where I test my guidance systems."
> "Here's my plating and painting operation."
> "Here's where I prepare them for shipment."
> One professor finally turned to a colleague and wryly remarked, "I wonder why this guy needs 6,000 employees? It sounds like he does it all himself!"

Qualifications, by the way, may have no bearing on compatibility and good chemistry between people and their jobs. I remember talking privately with several aerospace engineers who were students in a graduate management course I taught as part of an MBA program. Although impeccably qualified, these people loathed their high-paying jobs and were desperate to change fields. To them, an advanced degree was a passport to a more satisfying career.

What compounds your challenge to motivate others is the tendency for people to undergo a basic shift in personal preferences, interests, goals, and priorities every several years. Even agile managers shouldn't expect employees to maintain, let alone increase, the level of interest, enthusiasm, and ambition they brought to their jobs as years go by.

For example, you might hire a newly minted college graduate with a degree in marketing to be a sales trainee. Once out in the field, she goes on to set sales records for seven straight years, but gradually comes to feel, for whatever reasons, that she'd really rather work in human resources management, do hostage negotiations for the county sheriff's department, or work in a dive shop in Key West.

Meanwhile, there's a Key West dive-shop employee who secretly yearns to run his own charter boat, a hostage negotiator would rather breed Siamese cats, and a human resources manager who dreams of going into business for himself and restoring antique furniture.

I have one friend who has been, at various times, an attorney, a mediator, a novelist, and a preacher. His life was a work in progress (isn't that true for many of us?), and he was a fascinating guy to talk to. But he made a career out of finding a career, which is a personal trait that could drive some bosses nuts.

As managers and employees, then, we should be prepared to see formerly contented workers fall out of love with their jobs, because they simply change as the experience of living changes them.

This doesn't make them bad people or bad workers. In fact, they may be excellent, fantastically gung-ho employees in some other part of their present organization if only managers would help them become qualified for the kind of work they'd really rather do today.

Let's assume for now, though, that you believe you have a good match between your workers and their work. They all basically enjoy their jobs. What can you do that might cause them to invest more effort at work than they have to? We'll look at six techniques here and four others in chapter four.

Delegate Authority

When you delegate authority to workers, you pass down some of your job to them. At the right time, with a person who's presently well matched with the work, delegation can be a powerful motivating experience.

You'll find an entire book on the topic in the Agile Manager Series. We can say here, however, that delegation pushes at least some of the buttons on McGregor's, Herzberg's, and Maslow's theories simultaneously. Symbolically, delegation says:

- I believe you can do it, and I'm confident that you'll do your best. (This implied trust and commitment makes you one of McGregor's Theory Y bosses.)
- I'm giving you an opportunity to expand your repertoire of skills and develop inside the job you have now. (This smacks of Herzberg's motivational factors: a chance for the employee to grow and become more qualified for advancement.)
- This added authority is also meant to make you feel important and valuable. (You've helped the worker satisfy some esteem and perhaps self-fulfillment needs on Maslow's hierarchy.)

Best Tip
Delegate authority. It's a key idea in nearly every theory of how to motivate a person. Besides, it works.

Nothing gets people feeling important like delegation. Delegated work is, by definition, higher-level work than an employee is used to doing. Delegation builds confidence and helps employees acquire skills, experience, and insight.

Here are a few guidelines:

1. When you delegate a job, give it to the lowest-level person who can handle it. It'll be a challenge for that person, and the work is being done by the least costly person.

2. Say exactly what result you want. "I need you to figure out whether it makes sense to build a product for this market. Come back to me in two weeks with a recommendation either way, along with the arguments that support your view."

3. Don't tell the person how to do the job. That's not delegating—it's an attempt to clone yourself. Make yourself available for guidance and nothing more.

4. If you check up on the work at all, do it unobtrusively and infrequently.

5. Never take a delegated job back. Poor managers often do

this, unable to relinquish control. Another problem: Employees, skillful in avoiding responsibility, hand jobs back. Don't let them.

Enrich Jobs

Job-enrichment programs, which add more depth or "vertical loading" to jobs, are meant to give workers more control over what they do. Workers are responsible for planning, scheduling, and performing tasks, measuring how well they did, and making corrections or adjustments as necessary.

TQM (total quality management) programs have enriched employees' jobs in companies that have instituted them.

You may not need to create an entire job-enrichment program. Many of the motivational techniques in this and the next chapter add more depth to jobs, which gives several of them the flavor of job enrichment.

Enlarge Jobs

Enlarged jobs can provide greater satisfaction and meaning to workers by making them responsible for more than just screwing a nut on a bolt.

Downsizing has both enriched and enlarged jobs (for the

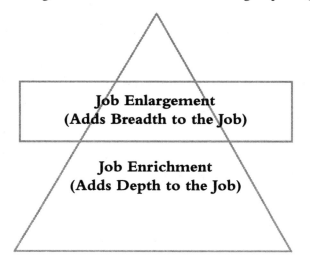

Job Enlargement
(Adds Breadth to the Job)

Job Enrichment
(Adds Depth to the Job)

workers who are left, that is!), because companies often consolidate positions when they tighten their belts. Layoffs necessarily broaden the scope of remaining jobs by adding more variety and responsibility.

In the early 1970s, Porsche engine builders were trained to assemble most of an entire engine by themselves using tools and parts delivered to their individual work stations. Likewise, I saw a classic Ferrari at an auto auction with an engraved plate on the engine's valve cover that read, "This Engine Was Assembled by [the Italian mechanic's name]." That worker's name and craftsmanship remained a part of the car for the rest of its life.

Rotate Jobs

Job-rotation programs can be motivating because they cross-train employees to perform a variety of related tasks. For example, workers within certain cells in state-of-the-art manufacturing plants may rotate among production machines and perform a variety of operations, including routine maintenance and service.

Department-store employees may be trained for and rotate among assorted jobs on the sales floor, in the stock room, and behind the customer-service counter.

Job rotation helps to reduce boredom, and it broadens workers' skills. That enhances their employability, job security, and confidence. It also gives them a deeper appreciation of the interdependence that exists among the jobs within their facility, work unit, cell, or department.

Job rotation can be good for the bottom line, too. It reduces the need for substitutes and temporary employees, and it can keep production humming during lunch breaks and other times of reduced staffing.

Show Appreciation

In one company I worked for, where every other day seemed to be Malfunction Junction, we had two standard mottoes: "You don't get paid for the job; you get paid for the frustration." And, "When you're right, no one remembers. When you're wrong, no one forgets."

Paychecks provide compensation. They don't provide lasting motivation. According to motivational guru Alfie Kohn, rewards should never be made an end in themselves. If they are, motivation becomes one-dimensional, because employees pursue the rewards for their own sake. Worse, management's reasons for offering them, such as improving product quality, productivity, or customer service, are overlooked or lost in the shuffle.

| Best Tip

"Applause is the spur of noble minds." Charles Caleb Colton, English cleric, sportsman, and wine merchant.

The simple act of saying "thank you" for a job well done can be productive for the "thanker" and exhilarating for the "thankee." According to a survey by the personnel consulting and recruiting firm Robert Half International, lack of praise and recognition causes more employee turnover than such factors as compensation, inadequate authority, or personality conflicts. Appreciation implies respect, which in turn generates loyalty, motivation, and a sense of self-worth.

Writing for the *New York Times*, columnist Adam Bryant looked into the conflict between pilots and major airlines in early 1997. Pilots for major carriers such as Delta and United Airlines flew sixty to eighty hours a month and averaged $125,000 a year.

A major bone of contention wasn't pay. It was recognition and respect. Pilots carry enormous responsibility for lives and property. During a midair emergency, they have to make split-second decisions under greater pressure than any corporate CEO may face in a lifetime. Yet they complain of being treated as little more than high-tech airborne bus drivers who are, as Bryant wryly points out, always first to arrive at the accident scene.

In addition to supplying one of Herzberg's motivational factors, managers who express appreciation for work well done are simply practicing common-sense courtesy.

In my first "career" job out of high school, well before the days of self-service, I worked as a gas-station attendant. The enthusiastic and entrepreneurial owner, who was an agile manager long before the term was coined, always handed out paychecks in person, smiled, and said, "Thank you."

Have many of your supervisors done the same? More important, how do *you* hand out checks on payday?

Mary Kay Ash, the legendary founder of Mary Kay Cosmetics, devised a spectacular way of showing appreciation by giving away pink Cadillacs to her top performers. She not only says "thank you"—she virtually waves a banner and gives her people a portable icon of a job well done that they can use to trumpet their success to the world.

Agile managers are goodwill ambassadors, morale builders, and perpetual thankers. They make it a habit to voice their gratitude to employees personally and frequently for whatever their accomplishments. They also emphasize how much those achievements mean both to themselves and to the entire organization.

Look for the good and praise it. Beyond that, make sure that others in your organization know about the good work your people have done. To spread the good news beyond the boundaries of your own department and staff, send in announcements to the employees' newsletter, write letters of praise for workers' personnel files, and so forth.

Reality Check

A top-performing employee who was passed over for a promotion complained.

His boss said, "If exceptional performance were all that I expected from you, I wouldn't have promoted somebody with inferior qualifications, now would I have?"

Ensure Equity

Agile managers are concerned about workers' feelings of equity—the belief that they're getting a fair shake.

Consciously or subconsciously, we're all highly attuned to equity. Expect employees at every level, as well as yourself, to make "equity checks" continually to assess how well they're being treated in comparison with their peers and counterparts in other organizations.

What do they examine? Inputs (what they bring to the job) and outputs (what they receive from it). Pay is a major player, of course, but they don't stop there. Workers also place a value on such factors as education, skills, experience, seniority, work assignments, personal charisma, and reputation.

They also look at the quality of their office furniture, desktop computers, employee parking place, fringe benefits, bonuses, and other "goodies" that management seems to dole out with some degree of discretion.

There are three states of equity:

- **In balance.** Here workers perceive that their inputs or efforts equal the fruits of their labors, and they feel content. ("Everything's cool.")

- **Imbalanced inputs.** Employees feel their efforts or inputs outweigh their rewards or outputs. They may respond by reducing their inputs (taking long breaks or lunch periods, sneaking away early to play golf, or goofing off). Or they may increase the outputs by looking for a job with better pay or benefits—or even stealing from the company and rationalizing their actions by saying, "I deserve this because of the lousy pay, benefits, etc."

- **Imbalanced outputs.** Employees feel they're getting more than they're giving. This may cause workers with a strong sense of conscience to feel guilty. Some may try to achieve balance by increasing their inputs (for example, working harder or putting in longer hours) while others may look for ways to rationalize and thus eliminate the imbalance. ("I may be overpaid, but so what? I've put up with this place for years, and besides, lots of other people in my department are at my pay grade, too.")

People typically have a keen sense of fairness. For example, one manager was asked by a friend whether he resented supervising a group of professionals who worked about 35 percent fewer hours per week than he did. His answer was no, because he earned about $20,000 more per year than they did, and the additional hours his job required were merely a trade-off for the higher pay. In his view, it was a fair deal.

If employees perceive that they're being treated unfairly or discriminated against, disclaimers or counterarguments by management will fall on deaf ears. They'll

> ### Best Tip
>
> Understand that employees will, one way or another, balance inputs and outputs. Lesson: Pay now or pay later.

look for some way to change the quality or quantity of their inputs or outputs that will restore a balance between what they're giving and what they think they should be getting. In the process, workers will register their objections and/or express their feelings of uneasiness through a variety of behaviors, few of which may bode well for the organization. For example:

➜ An employee who worked on a popular thrill ride at a major Central Florida tourist attraction (am I being general enough here?) told me a fascinating tale of inequity that caused periodic mechanical malfunctions.

"We work on the ride for days on end," he said, "dealing with sweaty, nasty tourists and their whining kids, while management acts like we don't even exist. When things get bad enough, we'll cause a 'breakdown.' Nothing dangerous, just something that will stop the ride for awhile. As the line of guests backs up across the plaza, supervisors come running down from their offices to find out what happened. They need us to troubleshoot what went wrong. They talk to us face to face, and we talk to them. They confirm that we're alive and that our jobs are really important. Finally, we locate the 'problem,' fix it, and get the ride up and running. The managers go away, and we feel better for several days. But as soon as we feel ignored or taken for granted, we do it all over again. They never seem to catch on."

→ One high-profile department manager who had come up through the ranks at a major manufacturing company was openly hostile and uncooperative toward several new college grads whom he had to show the ropes as they passed through a management-training program. "These college boys," he'd say with a sneer. "They come in here saying, 'Whee, whee, I've got a degree,' while I'm the jerk who does all the work."

His contemptuous behavior was caused by deep feelings of inequity. He resented the fact that management hadn't acknowledged and rewarded him for his hard-won knowledge and experience and made him be a mentor to these newcomers. In his view, their education eclipsed his seniority and achievements and may eventually qualify them to take his job.

→ One government employee who sometimes believed she received an inequitable annual pay raise in relation to others in her department had an interesting approach to achieving equity. "I just reduce my effort," she said. "If I think I should have gotten an 8 percent raise and it was only 5 percent, then I'll cut back on my work by 3 percent next year. I believe I deserve 8; I get 5; I cut back by 3. That sounds fair to me!"

Best Tip

If you take employees for granted and ignore their ideas, they'll find ways to make you pay attention.

→ On the high side, some senior executives (albeit not many) confess to feeling profoundly uncomfortable about the high salaries they earn in comparison with so many other members of

---

Reality Check

An auto service and parts center cleaned out old, unsalable inventory. After hours, some of the employees rooted through the boxes left by the curb for pickup.

Seeing what they were doing, a manager came out and said, menacingly, "I've seen people fired for taking home discarded inventory."

"But it's garbage," said one of the employees, holding an old tire-pressure gauge in his hand.

"But it's company garbage," said the manager. "Put it all back or you'll be out of work."

---

society. (One executive said, "My father raised his family on about $150 a week. I make more than ten times that much in an hour! Is any human being really worth several million dollars a year? Although I'm grateful for my salary, I sometimes don't think I really earn or deserve it.")

Their feelings of guilt about being so lavishly rewarded lead some to seek counseling through employee-assistance programs. Some also donate large amounts of money to charitable organizations as a way to achieve a sense of equity between what they are paid and the amount they suspect, in their minds, is justified.

➜ Outside the corporate arena, taxpayers who believe the government is using their dollars wastefully, irresponsibly, or in ways they don't approve of may defend fudging on their income tax as a way to achieve equity. ("If the government's cheating me by the stupid ways it throws away my tax money, why shouldn't I cheat back?")

In a nutshell, employees' motivation is affected by how they perceive their situation—what they bring to and take out of their job compared to the inputs and outputs of co-workers. Realize that different people have different perceptions that affect their sense of equity. Try to confirm and reinforce—through compensation programs, perquisites, pay, praise, and all other dealings with employees—the impression that everyone is being rewarded fairly and no one is playing favorites, being ignored, being discriminated against, or taken for granted.

Equity is, obviously, a key concept in motivating people. Pay attention to it, and it can eliminate many of your problems.

Major Programs Require Major Changes

Although delegation, appreciation, and (to a great extent) equity start with and are governed by individual managers, job enrichment, job enlargement, and job rotation may call for major changes in a company's operations.

- Traditional training programs and pay rates can't be carried over to enriched or enlarged jobs or job rotation. Training methods, facilities, and delivery systems will have to be redesigned to teach the required skills. Not surprisingly, workers who are asked to take on more responsibilities and enhance their capabilities will expect to be paid more—and they should be.

- Whether it's a manufacturing or an office setting, the old system will have to be modified to accommodate redesigned jobs. This means that the physical work layout, materials handling, paperwork or production flow, and communication and coordination among departments must be overhauled. An added benefit for manufacturing companies that have converted from a traditional production line to a cell system: You save space by localizing many related operations in one area.

- Old-school "I'm paid to think; you're paid to work" supervisors must make some fundamental changes in how they see themselves and lead their employees. For dyed-in-the-wool hard-liners, this may become an adapt-or-be-fired situation and a major culture shock. In many of today's offices and plants, downsizing and its consequential by-product, job enlargement, has turned supervisors into facilitators and resource providers more than close-to-the-workforce managers. Hence "hands-on" managers must face the realities of today and the challenge of tomorrow by learning to let go.

- Employees who are hired to work in enriched, enlarged, and rotating jobs must be resourceful, adaptable, flexible, and self-directed to handle the empowerment that comes with such contemporary positions. This adds a whole new dimension to a traditional firm's recruiting, hiring, training, and performance-evaluation functions.

The Agile Manager's Checklist

✔ To motivate effectively, start with a good match between employee and job.

✔ Delegate authority. It's a way to apply McGregor's, Herzberg's, and Maslow's theories of motivation simultaneously.

✔ Cross-train employees and rotate them among jobs. They'll be more useful to you—and more interested in their work.

✔ Consider handing paychecks out personally and saying "thank you" to each employee.

✔ Make sure employees are rewarded equitably.

Chapter Four

*B*eyond the Basics:
Proven Programs to Motivate

*"Money does motivate . . . but only for a short time and
only as long as it serves as a measure of worth
or of power or of victory."*

JAMES L. HAYES, CEO, AMERICAN MANAGEMENT ASSOCIATION

*"If you ask people confidentially what they want most in
their job—if they're paid anything decent at all—they
will say that they want a greater sense of self-worth. . . .
And I think this giving of responsibility and respect and
authority is one of the things that motivates people."*

FRITZ MAYTAG, PRESIDENT, ANCHOR BREWING CO.

*The Agile Manager caught up to Wanda in the parking lot.
"Your 'slacker' has been the last one out every day this week, I
hear."*

*"Yes," said Wanda, "and he even came in last Saturday. That's
a first."*

"So how's the project going?" asked the Agile Manager.

"Well . . . let me put it this way. It's an interesting experiment, and the outcome is uncertain." She pursed her lips.

"What? Really? What's the problem?" The Agile Manager stiffened slightly.

"No big problem, really. Just lots of little ones. Like for example he picked that dope Jake from engineering to be on the project team. And he seems to call too many meetings, which of course keeps people from doing the work." The Agile Manager suddenly relaxed his shoulders. "He hasn't asked for any input from me," she continued, "and he seems annoyed when I ask what he's doing. Oh, and today he sent me a Gantt chart for the project that looks pathetic. I'm doing a memo tonight that should set him on track."

"Hold on," said the Agile Manager with a twinkle in his eye. "All I hear you saying is, 'He's not doing it the way I would,' "

"Well he's not. And doesn't fifteen years' experience count for anything?" Wanda looked wounded.

"You told him the goal, right?"

"Yes," said Wanda. "I told him the most important thing is to make sure the product comes in on time and without any flaws."

"No flaws? Not sure I've ever achieved that myself. But listen," he said earnestly. "You gave him the job. Step back and let him do it! You'll know when he's floundering and needs help. Besides, we have regular milestone meetings, right?"

"Yep. I suppose those'll allow us to catch problems early."

"Right. Do what you feel you should do, but let me tell you something. A few years ago when you joined us, I had the urge to write you memos two or three times on how you went about your business. I never did. And I'm glad I didn't."

Wanda sat in her car a few minutes. Then she sped off briskly, having decided to see a movie that evening.

You and your organization can employ programs and techniques beyond those in chapter three to put motivational theories to work. And, like some of those covered in chapter three, most of these will require changes in an organization's structure or procedures.

Try Flextime

Flextime lets people set their own work hours, with some limitations. Although employees are required to work a minimum number of hours a day, beginning and ending times "float" so workers can decide when to start and quit.

For example, workers may opt to arrive as late as 10:00 A.M. or leave as early as 3:00 P.M. as long as they work the agreed-upon number of hours each day. The "band time" between 10:00 A.M. and 3:00 P.M. is when most business is done, so management needs everyone on duty.

If nothing else, flextime implies Theory Y management—"I'm giving you the leeway to design your own work day." Flextime liberates workers to take care of routine morning or afternoon personal chores such as:

- Dropping off or picking up kids at school.
- Running personal errands.
- Taking early morning or late afternoon courses to qualify for more responsibility or advancement.
- Recovering from or gearing up for some serious partying. (OK, agreed, that's not a chore!)

In congested metropolitan areas with many large employers, flextime has also taken a considerable load off public transportation by distributing the volume of morning and afternoon traffic over several hours. The concept is especially adaptable to clerical workers whose jobs require little or no interaction with the public, such as data entry or records-keeping employees in insurance companies, financial institutions, and government agencies.

Best Tip

Try flextime. It's nothing more than treating your employees like adults. In effect, you say, "I trust you to get your work done."

Flextime critics point out that managers may have difficulty locating employees when they have a problem or need information. Staggered working hours, further, make it hard for supervisors to meet with everyone in their departments at once unless the meeting is held midday, which is also the peak business period. Flextime can pose problems for work scheduling, too.

Overall, however, flextime's benefits tend to outweigh its drawbacks by a sizable margin. Flexible hours have raised workers' morale; reduced lateness, absenteeism, and the use of sick leave; and been used as a persuasive and attractive recruiting tool. Turnover is typically lower in companies that offer flextime, because workers realize that organizations that have such programs are relatively scarce.

Variations of flextime (which are often called "flexible work plans") include telecommuting, a four-day workweek, part-time permanent employment, unpaid personal leave, and paid sabbatical leave.

Permit Job Sharing

Sometimes called "twinning," job sharing splits one full-time job between two part-time employees. It often allows employers to hire people who either don't want to or cannot work a full-time job. These employees may include:

- Retirees, who often possess valuable experience, enthusiasm that belies their age, and an outstanding work ethic;
- Workers who are employed full-time elsewhere but want or need a second part-time job;
- Employees whose health or physical condition may only allow part-time work.

As far as theories go, job sharing may provide some of

Reality Check

Boss to employee: "I know you've been working here for eleven years, but have you ever thought that the saying, 'Nothing lasts forever' might apply to your job with this company?"

Herzberg's motivational factors, such as opportunities for personal growth and the chance to learn a new skill. Twinning may also help to satisfy one or more needs on Maslow's hierarchy, such as:

- *Physiological needs.* Some job sharers need more money to supplement Social Security income or earnings from another job.
- *Safety needs.* When employers cut back, workers who are suddenly unemployed may be eager to take any job at all, including part-time work.

> ### Best Tip
>
> Among job sharing's many benefits: Each "twin" brings different skills to the job—as well as fresh energy.

- *Social needs.* Retirees often appreciate the chance to get out of the house, interact with other people, expand their circle of friends, and stop hanging out at the shuffleboard court listening to their arteries harden.
- *Esteem needs.* Even a part-time job can help fulfill workers' needs to feel important, valued, and appreciated.
- *Self-fulfillment needs.* Retirees may enjoy the opportunity to contribute something useful to society instead of being "put out to pasture." Job sharers who aren't retired may gain more satisfaction from the nature of their part-time work than the full-time job they do elsewhere.

Florida's Publix Supermarkets has had an excellent experience with hiring senior citizens for part-time positions as baggers (or "front service personnel"—you get the idea). They're personable, reliable, cordial, and serve as good role models for many of their adolescent co-workers.

In addition to hiring some members of the work force that would otherwise be unemployed, job sharing enables each partner to bring to the job certain complementary skills or choose the duties that he or she does best.

For example, one person may handle the paperwork, and the

Reality Check

A nonprofit organization with a high opinion of itself sent around a memo that listed the typefaces that were acceptable for use in any company communication, including simple memos or letters. It didn't trust employees to pick their own fonts.

Interestingly, it didn't much care about what was said in these communications—only how they looked.

---

other will deal with the public. One may pick orders in the morning, and the other packs them for shipment in the afternoon.

Job sharing also tends to increase productivity. Two people who work half a day typically have a higher energy level and can produce more than one person plugging away for eight hours at the same job.

Management has to guard against at least one potential problem you may have thought about—the worker and the drone. If one job twin leaves a mess for the other one to clean up, there's bound to be conflicts and fireworks. In other words, both workers must be willing to work.

And frankly, many companies may adopt job sharing because they're not required to pay fringe benefits to part-time workers. The more generous employers, however, split many of a full-time job's benefits between the two job sharers.

Use Management by Objectives (MBO)

Under MBO, employees and their supervisors jointly set the employees' goals and evaluate their performances. The worker has input on the front end ("Here's what I'd like to accomplish in the next six months") and the back end ("Here's how well I think I did"). The boss plays multiple roles—coach, counselor, constructive critic, and sounding board—once both parties agree on what the employee proposes to do.

The boss and worker meet periodically throughout the work period to:

- Assess progress.
- Discuss ways to resolve problems or pursue opportunities that may have arisen after the goals were originally set.
- Revise or modify the earlier goals based on conditions that may have changed since they were first agreed on.

MBO is founded on a very basic and logical notion: People usually have more loyalty to, and will try harder to reach, goals they thought up themselves. If you've ever had a boss who tossed a list on your desk and said, "Here's what I want you to do," you can understand why MBO may be motivating for many people.

To succeed, however, MBO must be adopted as a *philosophy* throughout an organization, from top management to the lowest-level worker. An individual manager who decides to try it in one department or division is going to be out of synch with the rest of the outfit's thinking and feel like the Lone Ranger.

It can take more than a year to launch an MBO program and get everyone to buy into it willingly and implement it successfully. Logically enough, it begins with top management setting goals for the approval of the board of directors. Then the process is repeated at the next level, and the next, all the way to the bottom, where nonmanagement employees propose and set goals that their supervisors confirm.

Give employees guidelines, but let them form their own goals. They'll work harder to reach them.

This approach ensures that all the objectives are interdependent and mutually supporting from the top to the bottom of the organization. They complement and fit within each other like the sections of a collapsing telescope.

Like virtually all goals, the goals set under MBO should be expressed numerically. Quantified goals enable both the supervisor and the employee to measure progress and evaluate success objectively from one work period to the next, and there's no debate about whether objectives were met. For example:

Don't Say:

"Sell more products than we did during the last six months."

"Minimize the amount of scrap in the milling department."

"Deliver more shipments on time."

"Improve customer satisfaction."

"Minimize raw materials and supplies inventories at the White Sulphur Springs plant."

Do Say:

"Increase sales by 10 percent during the next six months."

"Decrease scrap by 3 percent in the milling department."

"Decrease late deliveries to less than 1 percent of all shipments."

"Reduce customer complaints by 20 percent."

"Reduce raw materials and supplies inventories at the White Sulphur Springs plant by 5 percent."

MBO is no magic formula, of course. Some companies have tried it and loved it. Others have tried and abandoned it in favor of more traditional approaches wherein employees have less input and involvement. Moreover, MBO poses at least one major challenge to even the most agile managers: How do you deal with employees who set absurdly low goals that should be a breeze to reach?

If you suspect a worker is trying to take advantage of you or "play the system," you can't just say, "Hey, don't put me on! Who do you think you're kidding?" If you do, you'll destroy the spirit and essence of MBO by reverting to the old "I set the goals and you reach 'em" system that's the antithesis of this concept.

If you're faced with an employee who hasn't set challenging goals, you may have to lead (and perhaps tactfully embarrass) the employee into setting goals that require a stretch.

For example, if business is improving, you might diplomatically point out that:

- The employee's suggested goals are on a par with or only slightly above the last work period's objectives.
- Business conditions have improved, which would justify the worker's setting a higher target.
- The employee has acquired more skills and experience during the past work period, which also favor elevating the proposed objectives.

Let Employees Participate

Unlike more formal programs, which may require major changes in personnel, compensation, training, corporate culture, or work layout, participative management is a technique that any individual manager can employ.

In essence, it's merely your personal campaign to become a more democratic Theory Y leader, one who resolves to let your workers have more input to decisions that affect them. A participative approach to management is, of course, a cornerstone of more broad-based programs such as job enrichment, job rotation, and MBO.

Don't expect employees to come forward with tears in their eyes the first time you ask for their opinions on issues or decisions. They'll probably doubt your sincerity or suspect ulterior motives. After all, if you've leaned toward the Theory X/autocratic side of management, it may take quite some time (plus hard mental labor, self-control, and willpower) to abolish a for-

Reality Check

A senior manager interviewed a candidate for a job. It being a position of responsibility, the candidate had a number of questions about it and the company.

The manager didn't like the questions. "Who's interviewing whom here?" he said, cutting off any more questions.

The candidate took it as an ill omen (rightly) and never followed up on the job.

merly dictatorial management style. You'll need to build credibility and convince workers that you're really asking them to play an active role in your department's decisions.

Best Tip

Get input from the people who will be affected by your decisions. They may provide eye-popping insights.

For many, this is quite a change of direction. If you continue to be a "my way or the highway" boss, however, you deny yourself the benefit of workers' experience and ideas, both of which may be critical to your department's (and perhaps your company's) survival.

Participative managers don't abdicate their authority and responsibility as leaders altogether, of course. Few if any organizations are run like pure democracies. When employees propose ideas or actions that are clearly not practical or doable (and perhaps downright harebrained), you'll have to step forward and say, "I don't believe this will work. We need to find another way." These are the times that someone's got to take charge—and that someone is you.

Money as a Motivator: The Fischer International Experience

As one opening quotation pointed out, money is a temporary motivator at best.

According to columnist Lindsey Novak of the *Chicago Tribune*, when Fischer International Forwarders set up business in the United States, two of the company's German-reared owners set out to provide employees with working conditions and benefits that were geared to encourage exceptional loyalty and motivation. These included a four-week vacation after one year's service, a 37.5-hour work week, flextime, profit-sharing, six months' maternity leave for either parent, and a host of other benefits from ergonomic furniture to health insurance that was 80 percent company-funded.

Employees' reactions to such astonishing generosity were neither motivated nor grateful. In fact, they were downright catastrophic. Productivity dropped; theft increased; workers came in late, abused their flexible lunch periods, and in some cases didn't work at all. Some employees were even contemptuous of management, interpreting the company's generosity as naive stupidity.

When workers ignored the exasperated owners' individual warnings to shape up, management cut back on perks and fired all but one employee. Attitude and productivity problems promptly disappeared.

Although this case may reflect some perceptual and cultural clashes (the pay and benefits that management offered Fischer's U.S. workforce aren't exceptional in Europe), it nevertheless bears out Frederick Herzberg's contention that hygiene or maintenance factors such as pay and fringe benefits only help to keep people from feeling dissatisfied.

The Agile Manager's Checklist

✔ Flextime and job sharing are great ways to satisfy employees who need time off to attend to personal matters. The organization reaps benefits along with them.

✔ Use management by objective to set goals and evaluate performance with employees. When you hold them accountable for reaching goals, you'll get superior effort.

✔ If you try participative management, don't employ it only occasionally. It'll take time to convince employees you really want their insights and opinions.

✔ Never forget: Money, great benefits, short workdays, and good working conditions aren't enough. You need to challenge people to motivate them.

Chapter Five

Motivate Yourself

*"If you think you're too small to be effective,
you've never shared a bed with a mosquito."*

ANONYMOUS

"Passion, though a bad regulator, is a powerful spring."

RALPH WALDO EMERSON

"Kites rise highest against the wind."

WINSTON CHURCHILL

It was 7:30 on Thursday night. Everyone had cleared out of the office but Wanda, who often told herself that it was important to be the last one out.

But she was depressed. She'd looked in on William as he was packing up for the night, and he was buoyant, as if he'd just risen from eight hours' sleep.

"Thanks again for giving me this opportunity, Wanda," he said. "I'm learning a ton and keeping everything moving, I think." He added anxiously, "Do you agree?"

"Yes, Will," she said honestly. "You're doing a great job."

And that's what depressed her. He was doing a great job, as were all the project leaders. Yes, she had a couple projects of her own, but for the past five years she'd overseen all the projects, and closely. Now she was letting go, which was the right thing to do.

But what role did that leave her?

Her eyes landed on the picture of her husband, always in the center of her desk. He'd just been promoted in his job and would soon be jetting all over South America to set up a distribution network. If she weren't careful, she'd get lonely and start to feel sorry for herself.

That's it, she thought, sitting upright. The picture of her husband reminded her how he'd always succeeded—by badgering superiors for more responsibility all the time.

OK, she thought, so I no longer need to be nursemaid to a bunch of product developers. I'm still the best project manager I ever met, and we have the innovative 3200 line that's barely begun. That's a line that could become a division in itself.

And I'm gonna get in on the ground floor of it . . .

How often have you heard someone say, "It's a lousy job, but someone's got to do it"? We've probably all felt like that at one time or another. When we do, it's time to throw ourselves the lifeline of self-motivation.

Self-motivation isn't merely important; it's essential for your survival. This ability can easily make the difference between excellence and mediocrity. In extreme cases, it can make the difference between having a job and collecting unemployment.

Up to now, we've laid quite a motivational load on managers and the company itself. We've explored some theories, looked at ways and means of putting them to work, and generally focused on external motivation—how you can try to motivate others who (recalling the key prerequisite) basically like what they've been hired to do. Perhaps the ultimate in agility, though, and certainly one that gives you a full range of motivational motion, is the ability to motivate *yourself* along with your people.

Put Self-Motivation in Focus

What is self-motivation? It's the innate capability to summon, without outside influence, the willpower to tackle distasteful assignments and do them to the best of your ability.

Self-motivated people are willing to sacrifice today for a better tomorrow. "Better," for example, can mean:

- Greater job and/or financial security for yourself and those you care about.
- Promotion to a more rewarding or satisfying position.
- Earning the freedom to move on to a project or venture that you'll enjoy doing more.
- Gaining the independence to start a business of your own.

If It's to Be, It's Up to Me

That's not just a slogan to inspire sweaty football linebackers and basketball guards. It's the battle cry of anyone with the desire to crawl out of the quicksand of adverse circumstances, whatever they may be, and move up to a more satisfying, independent, or rewarding station in life.

Self-motivated people don't see themselves as powerless. They don't make excuses. They don't wallow in self-pity or play "the blame game" for their situations.

Best Tip

Take responsibility for your present situation. Whatever it is, you got yourself into it. If need be, you can get yourself out of it.

Don't Count on Your Manager to Motivate

Wouldn't it be great if we could count on our managers to carry the motivational ball all the time? Ah, for such a perfect world. Occupational utopia. A cotton-candy dream!

No, don't expect your boss or your company to do the things we've covered earlier in this book unless you buy dozens of copies and FedEx them to the house and office each day for several months—something we encourage you to do as soon as possible. (And don't forget the board of directors.)

But in the meantime, many bosses simply won't or can't be as concerned about motivating their people as much as those people might like. Why?

- They may be so preoccupied with or harassed in their own hair-pulling job that they just don't have the time to look outside themselves and worry about their employees' feelings or situations.
- They may expect themselves—and you—to get the work done without any external cheerleading. ("If I can do it, why can't she? We're in the same boat!")
- They think of motivating as pampering and believe it shouldn't be necessary, especially when unemployment is high (as one boss put it, "I expect you to be motivated by

Reality Check

A shipping department supervisor found a dead rat near his office one morning. He wrapped it up in a sheet of newspaper and stuffed it into a small paper bag, intending to throw it in the trash in a few minutes. The plant manager dropped by his office, spotted the bag, and snatched it up. "You know we have a policy about no food at the desks," he roared. "I'm confiscating this as evidence; I'll check it out later."

"I don't think you'll like it," the supervisor said, biting his tongue to keep from laughing. "It's not exactly what they serve in the executive dining room."

"I'll be the judge of that," the boss said.

"I hope you enjoy it," said the employee, grinning from ear to ear.

the fact that you have a job. There are plenty of people who don't.")

Whatever the reason, you need ways to pull yourself up by your own mental bootstraps and get yourself in gear. Counting on someone else to do it for you isn't only unrealistic; it's professional suicide. Those who expect others to motivate them relinquish control over their future and abdicate responsibility for their own success.

When Is Self-Motivation Important?

Self-motivation is important in any number of situations, such as when:

→ You're working on a current project that you absolutely detest. The assignment itself, the people you have to work with, the fact that it was dumped on you ("Get this done by Wednesday or else"), or some other aspect makes you want to pull the covers over your head in the morning instead of getting out of bed and dealing with it.

→ You'd rather spend your time on other things, such as catching up on backlogged work, reviewing your personal-development program, taking the day off, or anything that appeals to you more than the job at hand.

→ You're confronted with a task that seems so massive, complex, or overwhelming that you have trouble putting it into focus and forming a plan of attack. It's hard to know where to begin.

→ You've invested so much time and labor in a project that you can't afford to back out and throw it all away—even though you may want to. The emotional and/or financial cost would simply be too great. ("In for a penny, in for a pound.")

It's pretty easy to identify people who have this self-motivational "X Factor." They're recognized as leaders in every area of achievement, from scholarship to sports and management to medicine. They're self-starters who seize the initiative and run with it faster than a pit bull after a mailman. If success is a journey, they make it a more pleasant one by becoming their own travel agents.

Have you ever worked with people like these? What a contrast to run-of-the-mill co-workers who whine, moan, and bellyache about their predicaments or circumstances! The latter group may blame everyone but themselves (uncaring/abusive parents, the boss, the other driver, jealous co-workers, etc.).

Best Tip

Find a role model that inspires you and discover what made that person a success. Use those practices yourself.

If they plowed all that energy into actions that would move themselves beyond their present situation (and get over themselves and on with their lives), how much happier everyone might be. So much for them. How about *you*?

HOW TO MOTIVATE YOURSELF

Okay, so you honestly want to move yourself off dead-center when you're stalled on, or would like to avoid, some disagreeable assignment or project. What tangible things can you do to find that helping hand at the end of your arm and use it pull yourself up by your own bootstraps?

Here's an inventory of techniques that can work for you as soon as you hit the office tomorrow morning.

Choose a Meaningful Role Model

Who do you know—or who have you read or heard about—whose success encourages and stimulates you? These folks don't even have to work in your field. All that's important is that they have "made it" in some honorable endeavor and earned a reputation as accomplished, respected leaders.

Pick one or more of these people to pattern yourself after. Research their careers and psyche in detail and answer these questions:

1. What sacrifices did they make to achieve their level of success? The only place where "success" comes before "work" is in the dictionary. Overnight sensations often take at least ten years. People who want to climb to exceptional heights of achievement are willing to make exceptional trade-offs to do so. What luxuries, conveniences, life style, status symbols, or short-term gratifications did your role model(s) postpone as they scaled their own personal ladder of success?

2. What productive, effective work habits and techniques did they employ? How early did they come in each morning? How late did they go home at night? How did they manage their time to get the most out of each hour? You could adopt a parallel work ethic. You don't have to reinvent the wheel.

I'm not suggesting, by the way, that you become a clone of your role model or adapt your personality to conform to his or hers. I'm saying that outstanding success carries a price. It's important to identify the price that your role model paid and be prepared to do likewise.

Let's say, for example, you want to be a successful novelist. How do some famous novelists work? One legendary horror writer claims to write every day of the year except for his birthday, Christmas, and the Fourth of July. A renowned spy novelist reportedly holes up in a hotel in a famous European city for one month to write each new book. He does nothing but eat and write during the day and go for a stroll around town in the evening. That system works for him. By living like a monk for one month, he can produce a novel.

Best Tip

Remember: There's no one "best" way to do anything. Use your role model's practices as rough guides only.

Other fiction writers swear to write at least five typewritten pages a day. Five pages a day will produce 150 pages a month (yes, except for February, you nitpicker) and about 1,825 pages a year. That adds up to a very respectable manuscript.

3. What mental attitude did they adopt toward their work? For example, were they willing to work nights and weekends when necessary? Did they see that as a sacrifice to be made grudgingly or an investment in their futures? How did they handle criticism (whether constructive or otherwise)? How did they react to and profit from setbacks and failures?

4. What leadership style worked best for them? Although there's no one "best" approach to leading people, which style was most productive for your specific role models, and why? If the same approach would be compatible with your personality and basic assumptions about people, what benefits might you get from adopting it yourself? What problems might it cause for you?

5. How did they manage their relationships with subordinates, superiors, and peers? Who were some of *their* most memorable and rousing role models? What on-the-job lessons did they learn, when, and from whom, that helped them survive and flourish in the real world? If they could relive their professional lives, what would they do differently?

6. How did they groom themselves for advancement? What kind of formal education do they have, and what did they have to forgo to acquire it? Where did they begin their careers? What positions have they held, for how long, and at what levels? What types of assignments did they aggressively pursue or volunteer for? Which ones were most valuable? Why?

7. How did these role models identify, create, or exploit watershed career opportunities? What techniques did they use to build a network of contacts, supporters, or mentors? How did they decide which opportunities to pursue and which ones to decline? What mistakes did they make in the process, and what did they learn from those mistakes?

Sounds like a lot of work to research all this? It is. But consider it your price to pay to sneak a peek at what's required to achieve success.

Pick and Post Sight Triggers

"Sight triggers"—anything you look at that causes you to remember your hopes and aspirations—represent many things to the self-motivated. They're a consistent cue, a burr under your saddle, a pebble in your shoe, a splinter under your fingernail, an itch you can't quite scratch. They nag. They chafe. They threaten. They promise. They're visual reminders of:

- Satisfactions or rewards you'll get from doing your job well and/or
- Personal, occupational, or reputational costs or penalties you'll pay if you do your job poorly or not at all.

The key to picking sight triggers is to choose ones that are as personally powerful, symbolic, and inspiring as possible. Then, each time you see them, they'll give you a kick in the butt—or a punch in the gut.

Post them where you'll see them as often as possible every day—on your bathroom mirror, closet door, car dashboard, briefcase lid, or personal computer. Their purpose is to keep you focused on what you should be doing to get from where you are to where you want to be.

Best Tip

Keep a photograph on your desk of the people who are depending on you to succeed. It's a great motivator.

Some examples of sight triggers:

1. Photographs. These can be pictures of people who depend on your success or had faith in you, material things you'd like to own, the kind of office you intend to occupy someday, exotic vacation destinations you want to visit, a location you want to retire to, or the storefront of a small business like the one you plan to own someday.

I know one female executive who keeps a somber photograph on her desk. It's of a destitute bag lady pushing a shopping cart. That sight trigger points out, for her, the grim consequences of missed opportunities.

Lots of things in my office are sight triggers. One of my favorites is a basket with several eggs falling into it. It reminds me not to invest all my efforts in a single writing or publishing venture, because I've been involved in the past with book projects that either didn't pan out at all or whose sales fell as much as 90 percent short of the forecast. Maybe all things come to those who wait, but it helps if you work like hell while you wait. And if possible, don't put all your career eggs in a single employer's basket.

2. Quotations. These can either inspire desire or predict where you'll go with the status quo. Build an inventory of quotations that have the greatest personal meaning for you, then paper your walls with them.

One of my friends believes that virtually all the wisdom in the world can be found in *Bartlett's Familiar Quotations.* Every agile manager needs a copy.

3. Symbols. These can be any objects that trigger inspiring thoughts or memories or represent positive goals or dreams: a letter of praise from a boss or customer; certificates of achievement; a model of a Dodge Viper, Ford Cobra, or Donzi powerboat; a mustard seed encased in Lucite; that filthy, unwashed sweatband you wore when you worked as a laborer the summer before you went away to college, which reminded you to make your grades and graduate.

Use Audio Triggers

These can be music or other material on cassettes or CDs that gives you a shot of inspiration on your way to work (play

---

Reality Check

A CEO asked a manager to encourage sales reps to feel free to speak up with their concerns at monthly companywide staff meetings.

When a few of these people brought up some legitimate complaints, the CEO cut off the discussion quickly and ended the meeting.

Afterwards, she ripped the manager to shreds.

"But you wanted people to speak up at meetings," said the manager.

"I know," said the CEO. "But not if they say anything negative."

Postscript: The CEO still wanted people to feel they could speak up at meetings, but she held the manager responsible for making sure nothing negative was voiced. The manager, who left a few months later, never figured out how to pull that off.

them in your car) and after you get there (play them in your PC's CD-ROM drive).

Many salespeople play motivational tapes to recharge their motivational batteries when they feel like a fire hydrant and everyone they meet is a dog.

And if you're an oldies music fan, as I am, you may recall such titles as "Workin' for the Man," by Roy Orbison; "Down in the Boondocks," by Billy Joe Royal; "It Don't Come Easy," by Ringo Starr; or "It's my Job," by Jimmy Buffett. These songs and others (stacks of wax from way back) provide a real lift for me when I need to get going. I either play the song or sing a line or two, and I'm on my way.

You have your own "platters that matter"; use them to inspire you.

Audio triggers can also be highly memorable comments that people have made—either to your face or behind your back—that drive you to excel.

An acquaintance of football coach Lou Holtz once said that when Holtz was in high school, his parents resolved, at great sacrifice, to send him to college.

Holtz met two neighbor women in the grocery store soon afterward and told them the news. Supposedly, as he walked away, one of them whispered to the other that his parents were wasting their money. Holtz's friend always believed that he dedicated his life to proving that woman wrong.

Best Tip

Use negative comments others have made about you—like, "You'll never succeed"—to spur you on to success.

The late Bill Lear invented the first car radio, the 8-track car stereo, the Lear jet, and scores of other remarkable inventions. In an interview when he was in his seventies, Lear recalled that as a child he never heard anything except negatives—that he'd never amount to anything and would always be a poor boy.

"I swore that I would *not* be that, come hell or high water," he said, reflecting on an exceptional career that began when he left home at twelve years old.

Do **Something!**

"Lead, follow, or get out of the way." Not a bad sight-trigger quotation, huh?

The only difference between inaction and stagnation is time. The longer you procrastinate or stew over an unpleasant job, the harder it is to overcome inertia.

When it comes to self-motivation, any activity is better than inactivity. When you face the dragon of an unpleasant task, attack it in small steps.

Best Tip

Get to work now. The longer you procrastinate, the harder it is to motivate yourself.

Gather materials; pick up a pen and a legal pad; boot up your computer; insert and label a blank computer disk; pull information off the Internet, out of your database, or out of your files; make a key telephone call; schedule a meeting; send some e-mail; or write a memo.

Do anything that gets the ball rolling. Action breeds more action. As it does, you gain momentum.

List Expected Benefits

Why should you do an unpleasant job well? Probably for several reasons, including:

- *You improve your reputation.* You hope that your boss will recognize and reward your well-done job (especially if he or she has read this book). That's another deposit to your reputational bank account. If your organization and supervisor respect and provide equity, they should acknowledge the unpleasantness of the task as well as its completion.
- *You may get more money.* The finished job may earn you a

raise, bonus, or other financial carrot at the end of the stick.

■ *You may get a promotion.* Completing the project may help to boost you up the ladder. At the very least, you'll improve your reputation as a self-starter.

■ *You'll confirm a Theory Y boss's confidence and trust.* When the

---

Reality Check

I recently toured a local business and heard the training director and several other executives describe the company's wholehearted commitment to teamwork. Yes indeed, this outfit was all for one and one for all. Just one big happy family. Unity and community!

On the production floor, however, things turned out to be a little different.

I noticed that the entrance to some departments had a large bulletin board with the manager's name at the top and a color-coded chart showing which jobs were in trouble.

"What's the purpose of these?" I asked the training director.

"Oh, that's just our management-by-embarrassment program," he said matter-of-factly. "If you're one of these team leaders and your team lets a key job get in trouble, management *owns* you. They've got your *soul!* Your life is *hell!* You can bet that every one of these managers wants to get rid of that status board. It's like having a sign on their backs that says, 'Next week I might be history.'"

Teamwork, eh? A motivating corporate culture? Employees working together with confidence and dedication? Yeah, right. This program screamed negative motivation, threats, and humiliation from every corner. It had all the charm and appeal of a flogging in the public square.

The hypocrisy of what I'd been told in the meeting room and what I saw and heard on the floor was incredible. Even more astonishing, the training guy didn't even grasp the glaring and bizarre contradiction.

job's done, you will have lived up to the expectations and justified the good opinion of a manager you respect.

- *You validate your self-image and reputation.* If nothing else, doing an unpleasant task on time and right gives your ego a boost. You can celebrate the knowledge that you've outperformed and risen above lazier, less-motivated co-workers and set yourself apart from the crowd. Cream rises to the top.

- *You eliminate the item from your agenda.* After it's done, you're finally free to pursue other more attractive jobs that will be much more fun.

Doing that tough job may earn you more money or a promotion. But do it for a more important reason: It gives your ego a boost and improves your skills.

Declare a Deadline

Setting and announcing a deadline puts your pride at stake. If you value your reputation, this is one of the most powerful motivating practices you can use.

Once you've committed to a deadline, you'll find that your attention is more sharply focused. There's a new sense of urgency, which will make you work more efficiently than otherwise.

Keep a Status Chart

It's no fun to chop wood unless you can see the chips fly. A status chart (you can find a sample at the top of the next page) is both a valuable way to monitor progress and an excellent sight trigger. It confirms that you're making headway, which can be important to your state of mind if you're plugging away on a highly detailed project where advancement is measured by the inch instead of the yard.

In addition, status charts ensure that you identify all details, account for important events and milestones (especially those

Status Chart: Opening up the East Coast			
	New England	Mid-Atlantic	Southeast
Route Map	✔	✔	✔
Contact lists	✔		✔
Appointments	✔		
Line up Local Support	✔	✔	
Travel Arrangements			
Go on trip			
Follow up			

A status chart used by a salesperson developing new territory

that are sequential or interdependent), dot each "i," and cross each "t." They're an excellent way to keep an entire project in perspective and note its condition at a glance.

Break Mega-tasks into Mini-tasks

This is the best technique that I know of for turning mountains into molehills and keeping yourself from feeling overwhelmed. It reduces frustration or helplessness about breaking the ice and attacking a monster assignment. If you split a huge job into a series of small ones and complete them one at a time, you're guaranteed to finish the overall task. It's as simple as that.

Let's say, for example, that you have a major report to write. You might break it down like this:

1. Develop a time line and identify key events. (Remember that status chart you just read about?)

2. Draft an outline of the topics that should be covered.

3. Identify sources of information.

4. Assemble the information. (Some of this may be delegated to members of your staff.)

5. Edit your outline, using input from staff members and other relevant parties.

6. Organize and integrate the information you've gathered into your outline.

7. Write a rough draft.

8. Edit the draft.

9. Develop and insert appropriate visual aids.

10. Edit the complete manuscript.

11. Send the report out for review and approval if necessary.

12. Rewrite the report.

13. Print and distribute the report.

The Agile Manager's Checklist

✔ Don't rely on your boss or organization to motivate you. Motivate yourself.

✔ Use "sight triggers" around your office or home to remind yourself why you're working so hard.

✔ Keep this slogan in mind: "If it's to be, it's up to me."

✔ Commit yourself to a deadline for a project or task.

✔ Complete any large job by first breaking it into smaller jobs. Attack them one by one.

Chapter Six

Build a Motivating Corporate Culture

"We have to get people excited about using their talents or we'll all end up going down the tube together."

PATRICIA M. CARRIGAN, PLANT MANAGER, GENERAL MOTORS

The Agile Manager looked around the room. He enjoyed these Friday afternoon parties. It was a chance to unwind and also to recognize people who had done really fine work.

He cleared his throat and then spoke into the microphone.

"Hey everybody? Attention here for a minute please. I've got a couple of awards to hand out. Get your hand off that tap for a minute, Manuel," he said with a grin. The two dozen or so people in the room looked his way.

"Wanda's gonna hand out the first one, but before she does, I want to ask you all to take a good look at her. You won't be seeing her for the next three weeks—she's heading off to the University of Chicago for some advanced work in finance and product planning.

"And why, you might wonder, is she doing that? Because you're *looking at the new project director for the 3200 series!" A few people gasped, knowing how important that job was. After a moment, the entire group began to applaud and stomp its feet.*

Wanda was taken aback at the sustained applause. She had to put up her hands twice to quiet the group. She felt great.

"Thanks very much. I'll miss you all," she said with a catch in her voice. "I have a special award here for a special person," she continued with a bright smile. "As you know, the revamping of the 1800B was of particular importance to the company. We had so many advance orders stacked up that any delay would hurt. But I'm happy to say that not only did it come out on time, but it nearly set a record for the fewest manufacturing glitches ever.

"That wouldn't have been possible without the leadership of one person." Wanda picked up a framed object that held under glass the initial drawings Will had done for the prototype. Attached to the frame was an envelope with a check in it. "That person is—of course—William! Will, please come on up and tell us all how you pulled it off . . ."

Agile managers who want to build a motivating corporate culture must start at the top and work down, because an organization's culture is the product of the behavior, attitude, and expectations of its top managers. These qualities are contagious. If they're not positive and exemplary, you're headed for trouble.

What specific things can you do as a person and policy maker to create and maintain a motivating environment?

Lead by example and set the pace. You can't expect your employees to expend greater effort or adopt a more selfless attitude toward their work unless you do. This is another argument for motivating *yourself* effectively.

Hire and promote managers who believe in being accessible to employees at every level. This attitude helps to prevent an "us versus them" atmosphere from taking root, as well as a dual culture of haves (the top dogs) and have–nots (everybody else).

A negative example from the political world surfaced during George Bush's reelection campaign in 1992. He visited a supermarket and appeared absolutely flabbergasted over its optical scanning checkout equipment. His amazement revealed that he probably hadn't set foot in a supermarket in years, which implied that he couldn't relate to the millions of us who have.

Managers who depend on reports and subordinates to inform them of what's going on down below alienate and rankle the rank-and-file.

Here's a positive case from my own experience. I had a boss in the textile industry who made a daily "plant tour" which took at least half an hour. He walked through every department, made small talk with various employees (he knew them all by name), and generally "pressed the flesh" in a pleasant, sincere, and genuine manner. Why?

- He wanted these workers to know he hadn't forgotten his roots. (He began his career as a low-level operator.)
- He wanted to take his open-door policy one step further.
- He believed this was the best way to earn the respect of the workers and demonstrate that it was mutual.

Face-to-face interaction helped him keep his finger on the pulse of things instead of relying solely on information from his department managers.

It was obvious to me that this was time well spent. It paid off in higher motivation and morale and a sense of unity years be-

---

Reality Check

Boss to employee: "I know you were qualified for that job, and you deserved to be promoted into it. But hiring an outsider saved me the trouble of justifying your promotion to everybody else in the department and to higher management as well. Besides, aren't you glad? This way your co-workers won't be jealous of you!"

fore the buzz phrase "corporate family" was invented.

Be up front with your people. Employees respect honesty above all and are quick to suspect a con job. Lies, half-truths, and ham-handed attempts at secrecy and deception breed paranoia, suspicion, and contempt for management.

Cultivate joint decision-making and the participative management philosophy that was covered in chapter four.

> **Best Tip**
>
> When you promote from within, you give employees a goal and a role to shoot for. Hiring outsiders, by contrast, demotivates the ambitious.

One company that had to pare its budget by a sizable amount took the problem to the people instead of sharpening the layoff ax. "If you can save what we need to save and still keep your jobs, fine," management said. "We'll listen to anything." Employees voluntarily cut their hours so that everyone would have a job, and cost-cutting suggestions came out of the woodwork. Because managers were participative and focused on the end instead of the means, employees were glad to help them reach that goal in ways that would keep everyone employed.

Promote from within. This policy builds loyalty and rewards (or should reward, in the absence of a union contract that promotes on seniority) outstanding performance. Its success, however, hinges on effective training and a performance-evaluation and management-development system that identifies and grooms your peak performers for leadership positions.

Give credit where credit is due. This goes beyond a two-sentence write-up in the employee newsletter. Individual managers must scrupulously acknowledge jobs well done and praise attitudes and efforts that are above and beyond the norm. People know when they've done well, and they expect to hear about it. Managers who steal credit for employees' achievements and ideas are unethical intellectual pirates who deserve to walk the corporate plank.

Do the right thing. This is another situation in which managers must lead by example, even if it's expensive, awkward, or uncomfortable to do so. One top manager who was a natural introvert met each month with different employees for a brainstorming breakfast. Although he admitted to being ill at ease, he did this because he was determined to foster clear and honest two-way communications. If he had to set his personal preferences aside in the process, so be it.

Roll up your sleeves and work alongside everyone else when necessary. Managers who do this earn employees' respect and prove they're not hypocrites who demand less from themselves than they do from their people. One Saturday afternoon in the fall, I watched a Tallahassee bar owner casually sipping a drink with his girlfriend, while his two harassed bartenders were run ragged trying to serve the rowdy standing-room-only crowd after a major F.S.U. Seminoles' football victory at the stadium two blocks away. This earned him the scorn of his employees and customers alike and a caustic objection from at least one of them (yours truly).

When it comes to pitching in, actions speak louder than words and say, "I'm not better than you; we're all in this together." Your enthusiasm and commitment aren't merely contagious. They also generate loyalty and reduce turnover by giving people a rea-

Best Tip

You can inspire loyalty and greater effort by getting in the trenches with your employees and doing real work.

son for staying on and doing their best. Said the employee of one such manager, "If that approach got her where she is, it'll probably do the same for me."

Make employees stakeholders in your organization's success through profit sharing, stock options, bonuses, and other tangible and meaningful rewards. When you establish a direct link between their efforts and organizational and personal prosperity, you create a system and probably a turnover rate that may become the envy of your industry. For example, one large manufacturing company with an exceptional profit-sharing plan often pointed to the fact that many retired employees made more money from profit sharing and social security than they did when they were working.

The Twin Pillars of a Motivating Culture

A motivating corporate culture rests on the twin pillars of (1) a motivating organizational environment and (2) the exemplary attitudes of individual managers. Which one comes first might raise a chicken-and-egg debate, but both are necessary if an organization hopes to flourish in the twenty-first century.

A CAPSTONE CASE:
THE CITY OF CLAREMONT, CALIFORNIA

Some of the employee motivation programs that were created by the City of Claremont, California, (Algird G. Legia, mayor) help to unite and illustrate some of the motivational practices and techniques you've read about up to now. We thank the city for giving us permission to tell its story.

Located in California's San Gabriel Valley, Claremont (population 33,000) is the easternmost city in Los Angeles County. Like most California cities, Claremont has been faced with the challenge of maintaining a high-quality staff and keeping employee morale high in the face of significant cutbacks. Staff has been reduced 24 percent over the last four years, while at the same time citizens demand that officials "reinvent government" to make it work better.

Responding to what many people may view as conflicting demands, Claremont implemented a series of innovative programs designed to empower employees in their professional and personal lives through development, motivation, and education. Claremont's employee-relations philosophy is pretty basic:

■ Treat employees the way you would want to be treated,

Reality Check

Boss to worker: "You ought to be glad that I take credit for your ideas. If they weren't so good, I wouldn't have kept you on the payroll so long!"

- Compensate them fairly,
- Train them well,
- Recognize their achievements and accomplishments.

The benefits of Claremont's employee motivation programs have far exceeded expectations. Attrition is practically nonexistent, employees are satisfied and happy (and therefore productive), and the community is very supportive of city employees. How did Claremont successfully meet the varied challenges of the 1990s? Through a number of programs.

Employee Development Advisory Committee (EDAC)

Claremont's Employee Development Advisory Committee (EDAC) was established in 1988 to serve as the city manager's "Commission" for employees. Each of the city's five departments and three employee associations is represented on EDAC. Members serve a two-year term and may serve no more than two consecutive terms. A president, vice president, treasurer, and secretary are elected from among the group to serve a one-year term, which can be extended for an additional year.

The entire group meets once a month. Officers also meet monthly with the city manager. The assistant city manager is the committee's staff advisor.

One of EDAC's early goals was to develop employee-related activities to help with career development and personal and professional education while encouraging employees to have fun and enjoy one another. Over the years, EDAC has established an employee holiday party, an annual picnic for employees and their families, quarterly potluck meals, an Easter egg hunt, activities for each day of Employee Recognition Week, a Halloween costume contest, employee service anniversary gifts, long lunch hours to attend movies and do holiday shopping, and ski days.

With an annual budget of $15,000, EDAC has sponsored programs and seminars on such topics as CPR, breast cancer awareness, personal safety, auto mechanics, home repair, family communications, drug and alcohol abuse awareness, and financial and retirement planning.

When the city purchased a networked personal computer system, EDAC coordinated the employee-training programs. The group has also sponsored employee attendance at off-site training programs covering everything from public works inspection to advanced computer training for employees who don't normally perform those duties as a part of their regular assignments.

| **Best Tip**
Alternative work schedules — like working four ten-hour days — can reduce absenteeism, decrease overtime, and increase productivity.

Concerned about earthquake preparedness and safety, EDAC developed an education program that included the purchase of an earthquake safety video that employees could check out. It also researched and purchased supplies and materials for emergency kits for each city facility. Each kit contains everything from first aid supplies to food, water, gloves, and masks.

EDAC has succeeded because employees are empowered to be responsible for themselves and their peers. Claremont employees have learned the value of having fun while they work together. They truly embrace the "Team Claremont" slogan emblazoned on their T-shirts, sun visors, baseball hats, and employment anniversary gifts.

Flextime and Alternative Work Schedules

Claremont's present workforce is very different from that of twenty years ago. Although most employees have spouses who also work, many are single parents for whom time is a precious commodity. Even though the vast majority of employees are dedicated and willing to do whatever is needed to get the job done, they often can't accomplish their tasks during a "normal" 8:00 A.M. to 5:00 P.M. work day.

Flextime. Recognizing these dynamics, Claremont implemented a flextime program. The plan requires non-shift employees to be at work during a "core" time of 9:00 A.M. to 4:00 P.M. but allows them to come in as early as 7:00 A.M. and leave as late as 6:00 P.M. Management learned that employees arrived and left at their scheduled time even without the watchful eye of a supervisor.

Alternative work schedules. The City of Claremont has no single alternative work schedule. Police patrol officers work a schedule of three twelve-hour days, while most detectives, records clerks, dispatchers, jailers, and community services bureau personnel work four ten-hour days.

In implementing the alternative work schedule program, Claremont's City Manager required only that:

- Services to the public not be reduced;
- There be no whining;
- Employees get their jobs done.

In addition to substantially improving employee morale, alternative work schedules have increased productivity and decreased overtime and the use of sick leave.

Telecommuting

The city's telecommuting program complements both flextime and alternative work schedules. Employees whose positions so permit are encouraged to telecommute up to one day a week. As with flextime and alternative work schedules, telecommuting has increased employee productivity and morale.

Additionally, employees who must care for ill family members or wait for repair technicians are encouraged to work at home rather than use vacation or sick time. An added benefit of alternative work schedules and telecommuting has been the city's ability to get closer to the Air Quality Management District's average vehicle ridership (AVR) goal of 1.5 people per vehicle. The city's AVR, which was once as low as 1.06, has increased to 1.25.

Home Computer Purchase Program

The City of Claremont recognized that employees need certain office equipment at home to make telecommuting a reality and maximize productivity at the office. While most employees had basic furniture and supplies, few of them had computers. Those who did had machines that weren't compatible with the city's system.

Best Tip

Reward exceptional performance. If you don't, your stars will move on to organizations that do.

Consequently, Claremont has twice offered workers a home computer purchase program. In the first phase of the program, 55 of Claremont's 150 employees bought computers. In the second phase, another 42 employees participated. In both phases, the city required a 20 percent down payment and financed the balance, interest free, through payroll deductions.

While management didn't expect such a large number of employees to participate in the home computer purchase program, the city has reaped the enormous benefit of having a highly computer-literate workforce.

Rewarding Exceptional Performance

Claremont not only encourages exceptional employee performance, it rewards and celebrates it through the Pay-for-Performance Program.

As part of establishing the program, Claremont eliminated automatic across-the-board, cost-of-living adjustments in favor of market-based range adjustments and one-time lump sum bonuses.

Recognition and incentive bonuses. Nominations for recognition and incentive bonuses are accepted from all employees. Bonuses may be any amount up to $750.

City Manager's Award of Excellence. The $1,000 City Manager's Award of Excellence may be given at any time. Recipients are selected by the city manager for exceptional performance based on specific criteria.

Employee of the Year. All employees who receive a recognition and incentive bonus and/or a City Manager's Award of Excellence are eligible to receive the $1,000 Employee of the Year award.

The success of these programs has prompted management to apply pay-for-performance to nonmanagement employees as well. This made significant changes in the city's employee-compensation program necessary. Employees now receive merit increases commensurate with their performance as rated by the city's annual performance-appraisal process.

Participation in Professional Organizations

Claremont employees are strongly encouraged to participate in professional organizations and regional activities. Management believes that involvement in these things not only provides workers with training opportunities but also allows them

---

Reality Check

A boss who considered himself quite egalitarian and fair was about to use the company washroom when he noticed a lack of toilet paper. He went out to the warehouse where it was kept and grabbed a few rolls.

He hesitated at the door that went back into the office, not wanting to be seen carrying toilet paper. He spied a lower-level manager working a few yards away. "Here," he said, thrusting the rolls at the other manager. "Take these to the bathroom near my office."

to develop a network of contacts in other agencies.

Claremont employees are well-versed on topics within their respective departments and citywide as well. Management feels confident when they go "out into the world" to represent the city at various events. Participation in these activities is one of the performance dimensions considered during the annual employee-appraisal process.

Training

Training is historically one of the first things to be reduced during budget cuts. Many of Claremont's neighboring cities have drastically reduced training opportunities, including conference attendance. Claremont, however, has continued to encourage training and attendance at conferences and workshops.

Best Tip

Don't skimp in sending employees to conferences, seminars, or conventions. The contacts they make and knowledge they pick up can be extraordinarily valuable.

The city offers three types of training: job-specific, which is budgeted in each department; non-job-specific, which is part of EDAC's budget; and general interest, which is also part of EDAC's budget.

Job-specific training includes standard training sessions. For example, planners attend planning seminars and conferences, recreation department workers go to recreation seminars, and personnel staff learn about labor law.

Non-job-specific training opportunities, which EDAC encourages and supports, are offered to any employees who want to learn about other municipal government functions.

General-interest training includes programs mentioned earlier (breast cancer screening, earthquake preparedness, etc.). All general-interest training programs are coordinated, sponsored, and paid for by EDAC. The City of Claremont believes that its efforts to train the whole person complement the motivation programs that are meant to empower employees. The more employees know about city operations and themselves, the better equipped they are to serve the public.

The Agile Manager's Checklist

✔ Stay in touch with employees at all levels. It sends a worthy message—that you care.

✔ Be straightforward at all times: Tell employees both good news and bad.

✔ Acknowledge the achievements and contributions of your people.

✔ Give employees enough information and responsibility that they can become stakeholders in the organization's success.

✔ Work alongside your people when necessary.

Chapter Seven

Monitor Morale

"... Attitude, to me, is more important than facts. It
is more important than the past, than education, than
money, than circumstances, than failures, than successes, than
what other people think or say or do. It is more important
than appearance, giftedness, or skill. It will make or break a
company . . . a church . . . a home."

CHARLES SWINDOLL

"Hey Wanda," said the Agile Manager breathlessly as he caught
up to her in the hall. "I'm glad things are going great with your
project." Wanda nodded, but before she could say anything, he
continued. "I've got a problem and need your advice."

Wow, thought Wanda. He treats me more like a peer than a
subordinate these days.

The Agile Manager started a lengthy story about dissension on
a team whose problems included rampant duplicity and backbit-
ing. ". . . and so the team is just falling apart. But no one's talking.
What would you do in this situation?"

Wanda cleared her throat. "Simple. I'd create a morale survey. Anonymous, of course. In the case of that team, here's what I'd ask . . ." She ticked off four penetrating questions about working conditions, supervision, team skills, and information flow.

The Agile Manager smiled broadly. "Thanks!" he said. "I knew I'd get something good from you—you're so great with people."

Wanda basked in the compliment for a moment, then went back to work.

Motivation is being willing to invest more of yourself in your job than you absolutely have to; morale is your overall attitude toward that job. Let's look closer at how they're related.

If you'll recall some of the most motivated people you've met, it's a safe bet that they felt upbeat and positive toward their work—in other words, their morale was high. Now think about people you know who, for whatever reasons, have fallen out of love with their jobs. Are these folks motivated to put more effort into what they do? Hardly. Trying to motivate people with low morale is as frustrating as trying to build a sand castle during a hurricane. It's an exercise in futility.

Workers with low morale won't be high performers. And until you remove the cause of their low morale, your attempts at motivation will fall flat. But don't let that demoralize you! The good news is, this chapter suggests some ways to monitor employees' attitudes and identify morale problems before they convert from molehills into mountains. There's one caveat, however. Don't expect to be Mr. or Ms. Fix-it for everybody on your staff. Employees who are mired in marital, financial, emotional, or any other off-the-job woes may need professional counseling to turn their attitudes around. Such things are beyond your influence.

You can identify job-centered morale problems, though, by using one or a combination of three troubleshooting tools: personal observation, information from various records, and morale surveys.

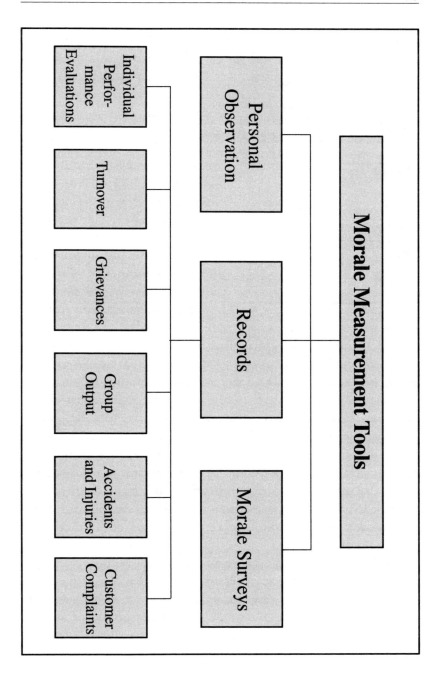

PERSONAL OBSERVATION

If you want to stay on top of things, don't isolate yourself behind office walls and assistants. Bosses who do that only get a second-hand (and often distorted) feel for their workers' morale. And if the underlings who feed them information are nimble spin doctors, they'll try to put out fires before the boss smells smoke, tell half-truths, or gloss over bad news. Meanwhile, problems may reach critical mass and blow up in everyone's face.

> **Best Tip**
>
> The records you're already keeping can help you spot morale problems and nip them in the bud. Review them often.

The best way to take the pulse of the people who are making the wheels turn is to go down where the action is and talk with (but most importantly, *listen* to) them. It's managing by walking around's finest hour.

Gather information through all your senses. Eat the food and drink the coffee in break-room vending machines. Would you like it as a steady diet? Does the noise in some departments hurt your ears? Could better ventilation eliminate nasty odors in certain areas? Are people using ergonomically friendly equipment and work stations? Is the temperature comfortable throughout the building?

Make it a point to talk to at least one person in each department. Pay attention to voice inflections and body language, including hand gestures, eye contact, and facial expressions. Does their nonverbal communication confirm or contradict what they're saying?

One seasoned plant manager who was a master observer made sure to walk through every department once a day. "I want our workers to see that I care enough to get out here instead of sitting behind my desk all day," he said. "I also go out of my way to exchange a few words with different people every day. That's so nobody thinks I'm playing favorites or have set up a network of spies back here."

This boss was great at picking up on signs of low morale. "If I see workers walking around with their shoulders slumped, heads hanging, and heels dragging, that often means trouble," he said. "If people who are usually cheerful or outgoing start to avoid me, clam up, or won't look me in the eye, I know there's something going on, and I need to find out what it is. There's no other way to pick up on clues like these except to get out here and go one-on-one."

The new human resources manager in a large retail store had the same philosophy. During his daily circuit through his store, he always asked employees, "Is there anything I should know about?"

This was no casual question. He asked it with 100 percent sincerity and followed up through proper channels to settle the gripes he heard. Before long, he built an excellent reputation as an ombudsman.

His concern paid off handsomely one day when an employee took him into the stockroom and laid out a complaint about job assignments and working hours that involved more than half the store's sales associates. They were planning to circulate a petition and take the issue directly to top management, believing that the indifferent store manager—who was about to retire—would ignore it. The HR manager met with the store manager immediately and, with some risk to his own career, described the problem's scope and severity. It was settled within two days. Personal observation, coupled with sincerity and superior listening skills, carried the day.

Some aloof senior managers conduct a tour of their compa-

Best **T**ip

Don't play amateur analyst. Help workers with personal problems get professional counseling.

nies' facilities as if it was a visit from the Pope. They're accompanied by an entourage of subordinates, lots of advance preparation, and much bowing and scraping from the local staff. The predictable result is that the people they meet during this highly orchestrated event are bright-eyed, bushy-tailed, and falling all over themselves to make a great impression.

Best Tip
Remember: You won't get high performance from people with low morale. Figure out the causes and act.

If you want genuine feedback, however, do what the legendary Sam Walton reportedly did. Leave your little name tag, coat, tie, assistants, and other trappings of your position at home. Walk into the place looking like just another casual visitor or guest. You're sure to get a very different—and far more realistic—view of how your rank-and-file people behave when they think the brass isn't around. At the risk of arousing suspicion, ask employees the following questions, and brace yourself for some eye-opening answers.

1. What's it like to work for this outfit?
2. What kind of training did you get before you took over this job?
3. How are the chances for promotion here?
4. Does management usually listen to your suggestions or blow them off?
5. What's the most frustrating thing about working here?
6. Does management give you all the tools you need to do your job right?
7. Do you have any trouble getting through to upper management from this level? If so, why?
8. Do you think you'll make a career with this company? Why or why not?
9. Are this company's pay and benefits competitive with others in the area?

RECORDS

Policies, procedures, laws, and government agencies require you to keep certain records and report this information periodically. That's good, because your in-house records can also be reliable barometers of employee morale.

You'll need a benchmark for typical performance or conditions in each area, which you probably have already. Material deviations from that norm will warn you of potential trouble. Some of your most useful morale-monitoring records are:

Individual performance evaluations. An alert supervisor will investigate a drop in employee performance ASAP. Don't put it off until the worker's annual review. Someone with a

When you manage by walking around, listen more than you talk.

morale problem may be long gone by then. Performance slumps may be caused by assorted outside factors, chief among them changing market conditions, acts of your competition, or a general economic slowdown. But don't discount possible fallout from poor communication with supervisors, conflicts with coworkers, a change in compensation, hours, or job responsibilities, or a transfer to an undesirable location or work team.

Recall recent conversations you've had with the troubled employee. Did he or she hint at any problems either on or off the job that may have caused the setback? If so, sit down and talk about the situation in detail. People usually need some encouragement to speak their minds. If you give them that, they may level with you about whatever's gone haywire.

Turnover. Increased turnover in some departments and facilities can be symptomatic of inadequate employee or supervisory training, limited opportunities for advancement, or unpleasant working conditions (which may include anything from substandard pay and benefits to poorly maintained equipment and sexual harassment by a supervisor or coworker). The best way to isolate the cause? Hold exit interviews with employees who quit and urge them to discuss their reasons. Follow up on their comments pronto.

Grievances. If your records show that people are suddenly filing more grievances than usual—or if their gripes are more serious or widespread than before—act fast. Higher turnover (and perhaps a union organizing campaign) is likely to follow.

Grievance reports should reveal which facilities, departments, or supervisors are generating the most complaints. Once that's clear, it's up to you to find the cause and fix it.

Group output. The quality and quantity of a group's output can shed light on morale trouble, too. In some cases, demoralized workers have even sabotaged production to get management to pay attention to them—reread the story on page 43 for a first-hand account of how that can happen.

Workers can also signal morale problems by a drop in productivity as well as quality. Complaints that depress an entire work team can easily cause a contagious apathy that bogs down the work flow without affecting quality *per se*.

Accidents and injuries. When you mix agitated or angry workers with inherently dangerous jobs, you've got a recipe for disaster. Folks who are preoccupied with or grousing about a morale problem are more likely to make mistakes or hurt themselves because they aren't paying attention.

One disgruntled loading dock worker, mad about a supervisor's arbitrary change in his department's work schedules, absentmindedly backed a forklift off a loading dock while complaining to a coworker standing in the warehouse door. The results?

> **Best Tip**
>
> Watch the body language of your people. It can speak volumes.

A totaled forklift, lost-time accident, worker's compensation claim, and an OSHA investigation.

Scrutinize the causes and circumstances behind accidents and near-misses carefully. What were the main contributing factors? Interview witnesses, and record what they heard or saw. Although poor maintenance, inadequate supervision, lapses in safety training, and other forces may be at fault, an unrecognized morale problem may also be the culprit.

Customer complaints. For every irate customer who complains about your employees' behavior, you can bet there are dozens of others who have simply vowed never to buy from your company again and will spread the word to everyone they know.

Analyze the sources of unsolicited complaints by letter, e-mail, or telephone and those made on in-house forms provided at the point of sale or by follow-up mailings. Summarize major sore spots on a chart that shows their relative frequency and week-by-week changes. Pay special attention to alleged customer abuse by arrogant, indifferent, or hostile employees. As with turnovers, grievances, and accidents, trace apparent problems to their source—the specific stores, departments, or workers who account for the lion's share of customer ill will.

Best Tip

Use a spreadsheet template to summarize information from your records each month. Examine all deviations from the norm.

Keep It Simple

All of this information is worthless unless you report it quickly, conveniently, and frequently to managers with the authority to take corrective action. Consequently, you need a miniature management information system that you can update with the least possible time and trouble.

Perhaps the simplest approach is to set up an Excel workbook with individual spreadsheets that summarize data from most of the records mentioned above. (The major exception, of course, would be information on individual performance evaluations, which should be kept confidential between employees and supervisors.) Review the data at least once a month, and examine major deviations from the norm.

A sample spreadsheet that reports monthly turnover rates for an office supply retailer with stores in three Florida cities and a workforce of twenty employees per store might look like the one at the top of the next page.

MORALE SURVEYS

Morale surveys are a more formal way to keep tabs on employees' feelings. You're free to ask as many questions as you want and go into as much detail as necessary about anything that may affect your people's attitudes toward their jobs.

Follow a Few Ground Rules

Like it or not, your employees will view a morale survey as a moral contract. Those who answer your questions truthfully will hold you responsible for acknowledging and dealing with the problems and complaints they told you about.

Here are some main ground rules to follow. If you don't, you may create worse morale trouble than you had before you took the survey.

1. Process and announce results as soon as possible. If you postpone feedback, people will assume you didn't care what they said or were afraid to confirm their criticisms.

2. Report all findings, both good and bad. If you announce only good news, workers will accuse you of being dishonest, which you probably were. People know when they're being conned.

3. Have someone with high credibility run the survey and tabulate the results. This may be either a neutral party (such as

Employee Turnover First Quarter, 200_	January	% Turn-over	February	% Turn-over
Orlando (Full staffing: 80 employees)				
Store 1059	3	30.0%		
Store 2110	5	50.0%		
Store 3231	2	20.0%		
Store 1419	0	0.0%		
TOTAL ORLANDO	10	12.5%		
Jacksonville (Full staffing: 80 employees)				
Store 915	1	5.6%		
Store 1101	4	22.2%		
Store 1812	6	33.3%		
Store 1998	7	38.9%		
TOTAL JACKSONVILLE	18	22.5%		
St. Augustine (Full staffing: 60 employees)				
Store 826	0	0.0%		
Store 927	2	66.7%		
Store 1005	1	33.3%		
TOTAL ST. AUGUSTINE	3	5.0%		
STATE TOTAL	**31**	**14.1%**		

Sample spreadsheet showing turnover rates

an outside consulting firm) or a non-threatening one (perhaps the human resources manager). Never let supervisors distribute or collect the forms. If they do, employees will be suspicious and defensive from the start, and many will refuse to participate. Who could blame them?

4. Keep identities confidential. There's absolutely no reason to ask for employees' names. You may, however, ask them to volunteer certain highly useful data such as their department and job title. Why? Because morale problems are sometimes concentrated in one or a handful of locations or positions. If you don't have tracking data, you won't be able to pinpoint the source of such complaints, let alone resolve them effectively. Make sure, however, to explain why you're requesting this information. People are bound to suspect your motives.

Watch Your Timing

The most reliable surveys come from a broad cross-section of employees who aren't responding under pressure or unusual working conditions. For best results, follow these guidelines:

- Do it in the middle of the week for maximum response. Absenteeism tends to be highest on Mondays and Fridays, and often it's these Monday/Friday absentees who have the worst morale.
- Make responses voluntary. Requiring people to turn in the survey as a prerequisite to collecting their paychecks, as one employer did, is carrot-and-stick manipulation.
- Conduct the survey under relatively stable working conditions. If you survey employees before or after a highly-rumored layoff, in times of rapid hiring, or on the heels of yearly bonus payments, you can expect biased results.
- Do it during the workday. Employees may resent being asked to fill out a survey on their own time. Some will drive home their point by throwing it away, which makes for disappointing returns. It's best to ask them to answer while they're on the clock; they'll respect you for it.

Suggested Topics for a Morale Survey

➡ Physical Environment
➡ Training
➡ Meal and Break Periods
➡ Compensation
➡ Benefits
➡ Communication with Higher Management
➡ Interpersonal Relations
➡ Work Assignments
➡ Promotional Opportunities

What Areas Should You Cover?

This is a judgment call. Generally speaking, focus your questions on the following topics, but tailor them to the nature of your specific organization and any latent morale problems that you suspect.

- **Physical environment:** Location, maintenance, and condition of machinery and equipment, and work stations; air conditioning and heating; lighting; methods of transferring materials, products, or information among departments.
- **Training:** Timeliness; effectiveness, and detail; relevance to regular duties and responsibilities; role in preparing for advancement.
- **Meal and break periods**: Frequency and sufficiency.
- **Compensation:** Parity with nearby competitors, colleagues who do comparable work in other departments, and present job responsibilities.
- **Benefits:** Time required for vesting; options (i.e., one plan for all versus cafeteria plan); comparison to those offered

by other local employers.

- **Communication with higher management:** Available channels; responsiveness to suggestions or problems; need for more frequency or detail.
- **Interpersonal relations:** Nature of relationships with supervisors, coworkers, vendors, and customers.
- **Work assignments:** Variety, challenge, and satisfaction; how and who determines; degree of influence or control over; contribution to personal growth and development.
- **Promotional opportunities:** Procedures for promoting from within; alternative or optional career paths.

No matter how many questions you ask, always provide enough space for people to expand on some of their answers or make general comments. It's possible that your questions haven't touched on a topic that's aggravating quite a few employees, and if so, they can sound off there.

Employ General Morale Builders

Most of this chapter dealt with ways to identify specific morale problems. But even when things seem to be humming along fine, it's a good idea to provide some general morale-building activities in the interest of preventive maintenance and overall goodwill. These might include, for example:

- Service awards
- Appreciation dinners
- Money-saving discount cards or coupons from local merchants and tourist attractions
- Discounted prices on personal computer systems purchased through one or more manufacturers or retailers
- Interdepartmental sports teams (bowling, softball, volleyball, darts, etc.)
- Academic scholarships for employees' children
- Employee-of-the-month contest
- Suggestion award program

The Agile Manager's Checklist

✔ Don't waste your time trying to motivate workers with low morale. Find the cause and fix it if you can.

✔ You probably can't do much about employees' personal problems. Concentrate on problems that are job related.

✔ Don't rely on second-hand information. Get out and meet your workforce face-to-face.

✔ Use morale surveys to gather specific information from a broad cross-section of employees.

✔ Use general morale-builders as "preventive maintenance" to keep overall spirits high.

Index